STUDIES IN COMPARATIVE POLITICS

The purpose of the collection 'Studies in Comparative Politics' is to provide the students of politics with a series of up-to-date, short, and accessible surveys of the progress of the discipline, its changing theoretical approaches and its methodological reappraisals.

The format of the individual volumes is understandably similar. All authors examine the subject by way of a critical survey of the literature on the respective subject, thus providing the reader with an up-to-date *bibliographie raisonnée* (either separate or contained in the text). Each author then proposes his own views on the future orientation. The style tries to bridge the often lamented gap between the highly specialised language of modern political science and the general reader. It is hoped that the entire collection will be of help to the students who try to acquaint themselves with the scholarly perspectives of contemporary politics.

S. E. Finer
Ghiţa Ionescu

Already published

Leslie J. Macfarlane: Political Disobedience
Roger Williams: Politics and Technology
William Wallace: Foreign Policy and the Political Process
W. J. M. Mackenzie: The Study of Political Science Today

Forthcoming titles

C. H. Dodd: Political Modernisation
Bernard Crick: Elementary Types of Government
L. A. Wolf-Philips: Constitutions
Ghiţa Ionescu: Comparative Communist Politics
A. H. Brown: Soviet Politics and Political Science
D. A. Kavanagh: Political Culture
S. E. Finer: The Study of Interest Groups
G. K. Roberts: What is Comparative Politics?

STUDIES IN COMPARATIVE POLITICS

published in association with

GOVERNMENT AND OPPOSITION

a quarterly journal of comparative politics, published by Government and Opposition Ltd., London School of Economics and Political Science, Houghton Street, London, W.C.2.

Foreign Policy and the Political Process

WILLIAM WALLACE

Lecturer in Government, University of Manchester

Macmillan

First published 1971 by
THE MACMILLAN PRESS LTD
London and Basingstoke
Associated companies in New York Toronto
Dublin Melbourne Johannesburg and Madras

SBN 333 13305 6

Printed in Great Britain by
THE ANCHOR PRESS LTD
Tiptree, Essex

Contents

1 Introduction

The study of foreign policy is a boundary problem in at least two respects. To the policy-maker, the political commentator and the student alike, foreign policy is that area of politics which bridges the all-important boundary between the nation-state and its international environment – the boundary which defines the nation-state, within the limits of which national governments claim supreme authority. To the student the study of foreign policy also straddles the boundary between two academic disciplines: the study of domestic government and politics, commonly called Political Science, and the largely separate study of international politics and diplomacy, commonly called International Relations. Both of these aspects of the problem have given a certain distinctiveness, and a certain peculiar difficulty, to the study (as well as to the practice) of foreign policy.

The purpose of this essay is to explore some of the features of this border region: to guide the student through the problems discussed in the relevant academic literature, with comments and examples to aid him where he may risk losing his way. In this attempt the crude and sketchy nature of the maps available, the thinness of the literature on foreign policy both in terms of theoretical approaches and in terms of available case studies, presents an awkward obstacle. A further difficulty lies in the extent and diversity of the terrain to be covered, in discussing an area which differs in its characteristics and its importance from state to state, in attempting to compare what some would regard as the incomparable. The nature of the foreign policy process, indeed the whole problem of foreign policy, is clearly of a different order in democratic states from that in non-democratic states, in developed countries from that in developing countries, in great powers or medium powers from that in small or weak states.

There is, nevertheless, a sufficient degree of similarity in the problems faced and the characteristics displayed to support an introductory discussion. Where characteristics diverge too sharply, the emphasis in this essay will tend towards great or medium powers rather than smaller, towards developed rather than developing countries, and towards democratic rather than non-democratic states. But many of the underlying problems, of policy definition, of boundary maintenance or of resource allocation, are faced in one form or other by all states. In what follows, the nature of the problem is first explored. The pressures and restraints of the international environment on states' foreign policy predicaments are then considered. In the third section the pattern of foreign policy-making and the definition of foreign policy goals and interests will be discussed. Section 4 discusses the domestic context of foreign policy, and the final section considers the impermeability or permeability of the boundaries which nation-states struggle, through their foreign policy, to protect. The essay is addressed more to the student of comparative politics than to those who are already versed in the study of the international system. But it may be hoped that it will be useful to both.

The separation of foreign policy from domestic policy is fundamental to the traditional concept of the nation-state. Domestic politics take place within the secure boundaries provided by the sovereign authority; the ultimate powers of decision over every area of domestic policy rest unchallenged (in theory at least) with the sovereign authority. International politics, as the word implies, is politics *between* states. Here states have no sure prospect that their decisions will prevail, and must contend for their interests with other equally sovereign entities. In such extra-domestic affairs, it has long been understood, only states themselves, only those holding supreme domestic authority and those authorised to speak on their behalf, can have political relations with each other. The state is the guardian of its citizens' interests, or of what is often collectively termed the national interest, in the international sphere, and the only legitimate channel through which those interests can be expressed.

The interests at stake in foreign policy are also fundamental to the idea of the nation-state. Protection of the national territory from foreign threats and foreign invasion, control of the national boundaries to limit the importation of foreign influences or foreign goods which might undermine the safety or the prosperity of the state, the continual and necessary assertion of its independence in its dealings with other states, are central considerations of national survival. The language of foreign policy, too, is closely linked to the language of nationhood and national purpose. Statesmen have commonly talked, to domestic and to foreign audiences, about their country's 'place in the world', or have boasted or worried about their nation's 'international standing'; while publicists and politicians have played on citizens' loyalties with references to their nation's 'way of life' and the need to protect it from corrupting foreign influences. Foreign policy questions, then, may be seen as too central to the survival of the state to be left to the same interplay of forces as domestic policies, too closely associated with the basic values of nationhood to be an appropriate subject for partisan debate and factional advantage.

It is hardly surprising, therefore, that foreign policy has been treated by political theorists, by constitution-makers, and by politicians as a separate and special area, which must be one of the first concerns of any government. For Hobbes, 'the right of making war and peace with other nations and commonwealths; that is to say, of judging when it is for the public good, and how great forces are to be assembled, armed, and paid for that end' was one of the essential powers annexed to the sovereign.[1] For Locke, 'the power of war and peace, leagues and alliances, and all the transactions with all persons and communities without the commonwealth' constituted the 'federative' power, which must 'necessarily be left to the prudence and wisdom of those whose hands it is in to be managed for the public good'.[2] In European states in the seventeenth and eighteenth centuries foreign policy was clearly a prerogative matter, reserved to the Crown. For the new states like the United States of America, writing their constitutions to guard against the dominance of monarchical power which they saw in Europe, executive control over foreign policy and defence was nevertheless considered essential to effective national government.[3]

This view of foreign policy as a separate and special area

of government, linked to the security and the fundamental values of the state, retains much of its force today. The constitution of the French Fifth Republic, for instance, begins its enumeration of the powers of the President by charging him (in Article 5) 'to ensure respect for the constitution', to provide for 'the continuity of the State', and to protect 'the independence of the nation, the integrity of its territory, [and] respect for treaties and Community agreements'. It also makes him responsible for the negotiation of treaties (Article 52), and even in limited circumstances responsible for their ratification.[4] In almost all democratic countries there is a widely-held belief that foreign policy ought to be insulated from the rough-and-tumble of domestic debate, that bipartisan policies should be sought by both government and opposition, that politics should stop at the water's edge; that continuity in foreign policy, wherever possible, should be ensured even when governments change.[5] Conversely, opposition to a government's foreign policy is commonly seen as more disloyal, more subversive to the state, than opposition on domestic issues. In almost all governments foreign policy is reserved to the executive branch, and effective powers are concentrated in the hands of a few men.[6] It is characteristic of the foreign policy process that a greater degree of secrecy, of concern for confidentiality and the need to avoid breaches of security, is observed by those involved. This in itself places a peculiar barrier in the way of the would-be student of foreign policy: that the practice of foreign policy is more shrouded in secrecy, that access to material is more difficult to obtain, than in almost any other area of politics.

The separation of the study of international politics from the study of domestic politics is reflected in the concepts commonly accepted in the two disciplines, the literature of academic study and the subjects chosen for study, even in the departmental structure of many teaching institutions. In studying international politics there has been a tendency to treat the objectives and the domestic environment of states as given factors. In studying comparative politics there has been a far more general tendency to treat the international environment as given, or even to ignore it altogether. It is hardly surprising, therefore, that the study of foreign policy, as 'a continuous process that bridges the analytical barriers between the international and domestic political systems',[7] has suffered from both a poverty of theoretical concepts and a relative neglect of detailed research. Loose concepts like 'national character', 'national interest' and 'national mood' still occur in academic writings on foreign policy, though long since discarded in favour of more precise terms elsewhere. There remains a disturbing lack of clarity, or even an active disagreement, among both academic students and practitioners about the definition and characteristics of many aspects of the field.

A preliminary difficulty concerns what is meant by the term 'foreign policy', and what areas of political activity it is taken as covering. For some, the term implies a stable set of attitudes towards the international environment, an implicit or explicit plan about a country's relationship with the outside world: 'a conscious image of what is or ought to be the country's place in the world, or some general guiding principles or attitudes determining or influencing decisions on specific issues'.[8] It was in this sense that General de Gaulle could accuse the Fourth Republic of having no foreign policy – no clear conception of its aims in international politics, or of the means by which to achieve them. For others, the term implies rather a field of related but distinct actions and issues, in which 'there neither is nor can be foreign policy in general';[9] in which policy is formulated in a disjointed fashion, largely in response to immediate pressures and events, in a number of separate structures and issue areas. Those who hold the former view, of foreign policy as 'high policy', are concerned primarily with diplomacy and the threat (and occasional use) of force as characteristic forms of foreign policy behaviour, to which a number of other areas of foreign relations are or may on occasion be subordinated. Those who hold the latter view, noting that wars or threats of force are exceptional rather than normal events in international relations, and that political calculations cover a much wider range of a country's foreign relations than national security and territorial integrity, are inclined to include in their definition of foreign policy commercial relations, the regulation of international commerce and travel, emigration and immigration, cultural policy, external investment and so on. This raises a difficult problem of definition which we will reserve for fuller discussion later. It will suffice here to note that one's definition of whether some aspect of a country's foreign relations is or is not political is largely subjective; depending on one's view of the structure and pattern of policy-making in that country, or one's appreciation of its political impact on the foreign countries affected.[10]

A second difficulty concerns the definition of the actors in international politics. We commonly talk about international politics as the politics of states themselves; we refer to Russian foreign policy, or America's attitude towards China. 'For almost all intents and purposes the state acts for the society internationally, and internal matters relating to foreign affairs are a state prerogative.'[11] Foreign ministers and ambassadors act in the name of the state, and deal with representatives of other states. Yet to talk of 'states' as such is clearly too crude, and leads easily to mistaken assumptions about the bases of foreign states' behaviour.[12] Governments make foreign policy in the context of domestic as well as international pressures; we must therefore look at the institutional structure by which governments make and implement their foreign policies, and arguably at the whole domestic political process as it affects their policy-making. Description of international politics as politics between states also obscures the extent to which organisations other than governments effectively act politically in the international arena. Stalin, for instance, is said to have dismissed the Vatican's claim to international authority with the derisive question 'How many divisions has the Pope?' But military force is not the only available resource in international politics; and it is hard to deny that the Roman Catholic Church has on occasion been an effective source of political influence and initiative. Other international religious and social bodies, international companies and arguably some international organisations also on occasion deal direct with national governments as effectively independent sources of initiative.

A third area of uncertainty concerns the objectives which governments follow, or should follow, in conducting foreign policy. For some writers, the goals of foreign policy-makers are clear and simply defined. 'Whatever the ultimate aims of international politics, power is always the immediate aim.

Statesmen and peoples may ultimately seek freedom, security, prosperity or power itself. . . . But whenever they strive to realise their goal by means of international politics, they do so by striving for power.'[13] States, these writers argue, pursue their national interest in foreign policy, and their national interest can be defined as the maximisation of national power. For others, the pattern of objectives which policy-makers pursue are considerably more complicated, and generally a good deal less coherent. Considerations of prestige, economic gain and domestic advantage, as well as of national security, form part of 'that apparently single thing, the country's foreign policy'.[14] It is therefore more appropriate, to these writers, to talk of interests rather than of a single national interest; to look for a number of separate and often conflicting objectives rather than for a single overriding operational goal.

A fourth area of disagreement concerns the relationship between foreign policy and the domestic political process. 'In the traditional conception . . . the domestic structure is taken as given; foreign policy begins where domestic policy ends.'[15] Foreign policy is assumed to be, at least in stable and well-governed states, an executive function, in the making of which the normal pattern of domestic political conflict plays little part. The importance writers place on the role of domestic politics in the formation of foreign policy depends partly on whether they approach their subject from the viewpoint of its role within the national political system or within the international system. Those who treat the subject as an aspect of international politics tend, partly in order to contain the spread of what they must cover, to limit their attention to governments and foreign offices, and to regard the domestic context as one of the background factors to policy-making.[16] Students of foreign policy-making from the viewpoint of 'the role the domestic social and political environment plays in influencing, perhaps determining, foreign policy'[17] tend to see partisan conflict, interest-group pressure and élite opinion as rather more central to the formulation of policy in this area. Not surprisingly, the former are rather more inclined to look for (and often to find) continuity and coherence in a country's foreign policy, and the latter more inclined to discern compromise and incoherence. There is a parallel here with the tendency of statesmen and journalists to assume that the actions of other states are entirely the responsibility of their foreign offices, even though they appreciate the diverse and often uncoordinated domestic origins of their own country's actions abroad; or to interpret the actions of other states (the Soviet Union, for instance, as seen by many Western policy-makers) as part of a coherent long-term plan, while they see their own policy as a series of poorly co-ordinated reactions to immediate crises.

There is a further disagreement over the degree of similarity or distinctiveness between the foreign policy process and the domestic political process. For some writers the difficult and uncertain process of 'implementing' foreign policy in the international arena sharply distinguishes governmental activity in this field from the more certain 'execution' of domestic policy.[18] For others the delicacy of touch and expertise which are particularly needed in the foreign policy area, and the unhappy experience of public involvement and intervention in foreign policy-making in democratic countries, require its separation and insulation from the domestic process. Others discern a pattern of convergence, in which 'as foreign affairs have increasingly commanded the attention of government, foreign and domestic problems have taken on a greater similarity', with the result that 'foreign policy has acquired the attributes of domestic policy'.[19]

A still further disagreement concerns the relationship between foreign policy and the domestic politics of other states. Students of comparative politics commonly write about national political systems as if they were almost unaffected by external influences. Almond and Coleman's conceptual framework for the comparison of national systems does not include any variable dealing with external influence or behaviour.[20] Yet foreign intervention in the domestic political process, and domestic awareness of foreign states' interest in internal political decisions, are ancient phenomena in national politics; and writers on foreign policy are coming increasingly to look for links between the external policy of a state and foreign influences on its domestic political process.

Behind many of these disagreements lie differing conceptions of the character and development of the contemporary international system. Some observers are impressed with the strength of forces for change in the international system, and see the dominance of international politics by nation-states, or even the viability of nation-states as systems controlling the flow of political relations across their boundaries, as being progressively weakened. Others are more impressed by the stability of the international system and the continuing vitality of the autonomous state, and conclude that 'the existing historical system of states will not be much modified, let alone superseded, in our time'.[21] One's view of the nature of the external environment and the permeability or impermeability of national boundaries clearly must affect one's interpretation of the factors which influence the making of foreign policy.

One last area of disagreement may be mentioned, over the utility or non-utility of recent theoretical developments in the study and analysis of foreign policy to the policy-maker himself. Much of the impetus behind the development of the discipline of international politics has been to improve the effectiveness, or the far-sightedness (or, for some, the moral quality), of national policy-making in this field, stimulated by the policy-making failures which contributed to the outbreak of the First and Second World Wars, and by the development of nuclear weapons as an overwhelming threat to the survival of states and of the whole international system.[22] Developments in the study of large organisations and of the administrative process, aided in recent years by the advent of the computer and the consequent ability to store and analyse large quantities of data, have provided new theoretical frameworks for the examination of the policy-making process and of the options open to the policy-maker. Most governments remain largely unaware of these new insights, and few foreign offices have yet made use of them at all. Their academic advisers are divided on whether governments would be wiser to adopt new methods to any degree, or to be content with more well-tried and traditional methods of policy-making.

It must be emphasised that it is not only academics who are divided in their understanding of the nature of foreign policy and of the international system. Their differing conceptions are mirrored in the divergent attitudes of the policy-makers themselves. President de Gaulle's opposition to the Kennedy

Administration's plans for Atlantic co-operation, and to the kind of European community towards which Dutch, Belgian and German policy-makers were moving, was not based simply on a narrow or nationalistic view of French interests: it was rooted also in a conception of the international system and of the interests of states which differed in several important respects from the assumptions which guided American and other policy-makers. Similarly, the current British debate over the advantages or disadvantages of entry into the European Community revolves, at bottom, as much around differing conceptions of the significance of changes in the international system and the possibility (or impossibility) of pursuing an effective and independent foreign policy outside the Community as much as it revolves around calculations of economic advantage. The 'reality' which academics and policy-makers perceive, of the viability or non-viability of the nation-state, of the underlying continuity or transformation of the contemporary international system, or of the relationship between domestic politics and foreign policy, is itself a matter of dispute. The remainder of this essay attempts to set out some of the main areas of debate.

2 The International Environment

Foreign policy may be seen either as a state's policy towards its international environment, or as a part of that international environment – a factor, among others, in the international system. The characteristic which distinguishes *foreign* policy from *domestic* policy is that it is intended to affect, and is limited by, factors outside the national political system as well as within it. Students of foreign policy are all agreed in stressing the importance of the international environment in limiting the choice of alternatives available to policy-makers. They are not agreed, however, on how compelling the pressures of external circumstances are – to what extent a nation's foreign policy is determined by its external position, to what extent still open to choice or to manœuvre – or on the weight that should be given to external, as opposed to internal, factors in the making of foreign policy.

Determinist interpretations of a state's alternatives in foreign policy, based on geopolitical or Marxist views of international politics, are now largely discredited. Of contemporary writers the 'realist' school, whose best-known representative is Hans Morgenthau, comes nearest to a determinist interpretation, based on their understanding of the nature of the international system and of the forces that move states.[23] Most other writers on international politics consider the external situation a more compelling factor in the formulation of foreign policy than domestic pressures: if not determining the course of policy, then at least severely limiting the options open to the policy-maker. 'The eternal experience of Ministers is to find that their choices are predetermined', above all by 'the intractable facts of international life'. 'Effective freedom in foreign affairs . . . is capacity to choose between relatively few options.'[24]

It is the compelling force of the international environment, and the slow-changing characteristics of that environment, which are seen as largely accounting for the stability and continuity of foreign policy. Others, particularly those who approach the subject from the point of view of national case studies, are more inclined to balance external and internal factors, and to stress that foreign policy decisions 'are products of internal responses to both external factors and domestic political considerations operating in dynamic interrelation or as discrete variables'.[25]

The international environment limits the policy-maker's choices in a number of ways. A state's geographical position is the most permanent limiting factor. No British government over the last four hundred years has been able to ignore the importance of the Channel approaches to British security; successive governments have therefore taken a close interest in the control of the Low Countries. For France the lack of a secure natural boundary to the north and east, and for Russia the lack of a secure natural boundary to the west, made concern with the Rhineland and with Poland a central and enduring feature of their foreign policies. The power of other states – their population, military and economic strength, their control of vital natural resources – and the balance of national power in the international system are also strong and relatively stable limiting factors. For France the population and the economic and military potential of Germany made relations with Germany the crucial problem of her foreign policy. For the Soviet Union the population and potential of China, facing the relatively empty regions of Siberia, imply a concern with Chinese foreign policy prior to and transcending ideological considerations.[26] Less permanent limiting factors include the attitudes and outlook of other states towards the international system and towards the state itself: amenable to influence, subject to change, but still relatively stable and slow-changing. The foreign policy attitudes of other states are, of necessity, crucial factors in the external situation which faces any policy-maker.[27]

These environmental factors, it is argued, alone severely limit the strategic choices open to policy-makers. The economic exhaustion of Europe at the end of the Second World War, together with the foreign policy outlook of the Soviet Union, created a situation in which the United States, for instance, 'simply had to fill the vacuum. The freedom of choice President Truman had was strictly limited: it concerned the moment and the manner in which America's taking up the challenge would be demonstrated.'[28]

If geography and the resources and foreign policy attitudes of other states limit the range of strategic choice, other less permanent external factors limit the range of immediate choices open to the policy-maker. The Hobbesian view of the international environment as a state of anarchy without any societal restraints has few adherents today; the 'realist' school, with their pessimistic view of human nature and politics, are the most disillusioned about the strength of international restraints on national behaviour.[29] For most writers the international system can be better characterised as a society, primitive perhaps, but with understood and largely obeyed customs and rules acting as restraints upon national policy-makers.[30] The social restraints provided by the international system may be grouped under three headings: international opinion, or 'world opinion'; international mores, or shared values on acceptable and unacceptable behaviour; and international law.

The idea of international public opinion as a positive and independent global force was widely received by statesmen and students in the years after the First World War. The Second World War, and the unsuccessful attempts of both sides in the Cold War to appeal to 'the good sense of mankind' against the stupidity or villainy of governments, have almost driven the concept out of academic discourse. 'Modern history has not recorded an instance of a government having been deterred from some foreign policy by the spontaneous reaction of a supra-national public opinion.'[31] Yet it is difficult to deny that generally-held conceptions of acceptable and unacceptable international behaviour do act as restraints on foreign policies, or that these conceptions change considerably over time. At the height of the nineteenth-century scramble for empire, for instance, the acquisition of colonies was considered a legitimate and prestigious foreign policy objective; the retention of colonial territory, even the attempted retention of colonial influence in formally independent states, is now considered improper by almost all states. This change in international mores has come about partly through developments in domestic attitudes in the leading states, partly through a revolution in the attitudes of the former colonial peoples, and partly through the positive efforts of states to affect the climate of international opinion over a long period.[32] If certain conceptions of acceptable behaviour act as restraints at the global level, even during a period of acute international conflict between groups of states with sharply differing values, then it is to be expected that similar conceptions should act more powerfully at the regional level: both because shared values and a sense of community are likely to be higher, and because a higher level of interdependence makes sanctions short of war more readily available. Public opinion in the Netherlands or Denmark is likely to have greater effect, through their governments, on the policies of Greece or Spain, for instance, than it will have on those of Brazil; not only because the widely-accepted belief in a European 'community' gives to both sides a greater sense of common involvement, but also because Greece and Spain stand to lose both prestige and economic advantage from exclusion from the European community. 'Moral restraints clearly operate much more effectively in the relations among friends and allies than among adversaries',[33] or among states whose range of contacts is more limited.

The role of international law as setting limits to foreign policy alternatives is rather clearer – though emphases differ as to whether it is honoured more in the breach than in the observance, depending on whether writers are more concerned with the day-to-day transactions of international affairs or with those less regular but more vital transactions which involve the threat or the use of force.[34] 'International law gets its sanction – that is, the equivalent of a significant probability of enforcement – from the significant probable cost of breaking it.'[35] The degree of mutual advantage which states derive from observance of common rules provides a powerful inhibition against ignoring those rules; though states naturally do their best to interpret the rules in the most favourable light for their own interests.

A further source of external restraints is to be found in a

state's external commitments: its alliances and treaty obligations, its foreign investment and trading interests, its citizens resident abroad. The wider a state's foreign commitments, the more limited is its freedom of action in foreign policy; its involvement and interest in the existing international system make it necessarily a defender of the *status quo*.[36] Conversely a state without extensive foreign interests is much freer to pursue destabilising, or 'aggressive', foreign policies.

Yet it is too simple to say that these restraints are wholly determining. It may be, as some writers suggest, that they set narrow bounds to the foreign policy states *ought* to pursue; but observably states have often ignored these limits. It is, rather, that there are larger risks and costs involved in ignoring restraints than in working within them. The United States did not, in any ultimate sense, *have* to take on a world role in 1947; but the risks of not doing so seemed, to American policy-makers, to be far greater to American interests abroad and to the stability of the international system than were the domestic costs of reversing the run-down of her armed services and retaining a large defence budget. Considerations of domestic advantage may, on occasion, override external restraints. In 1964 the British government broke regional and global treaty obligations by imposing a 15 per cent surcharge on imports, taking the risk that this would damage its relations with its trading partners in order to achieve what British policy-makers considered a more important domestic gain, in giving the national economy temporary protection. External restraints, then, are balanced against domestic restraints in the formulation of foreign policy. What direction of policy is in the national interest in any specific situation is not determined by the international environment, but remains to be decided by those responsible for policy.

The policy-maker's view of the restraints placed upon him by the international environment will naturally be influenced by his interpretation of the basic characteristics of that environment. The predominant contemporary conceptions of the characteristics of the international system are rooted in the international system of the eighteenth and nineteenth centuries: a system of sovereign states within secure national boundaries, whose political relations were characterised by diplomacy, limited war, and occasional aspects of trade – in contrast to the medieval international system, based on hierarchical loyalties, often overlapping each other, within the single entity of Christendom, concerned as much with questions of religious orthodoxy, or legitimacy or personal succession, as with occasional diplomacy or trade. Underlying changes, in the development of urbanised and educated industrial societies, with consequent mass involvement in domestic politics; in economic growth and technological development, with the consequent emergence of an interdependent international economy and with interconnected revolutions in transport, in communications, in weaponry and warfare; in the expansion of Europe and the revolt of the non-European world, with the consequent development, for the first time in history, of a fully global international system; these have transformed the basis of the international system in the last century.[37] Yet the forms of the nineteenth-century system, sovereign states interacting through diplomacy, remain. The problem, for policy-makers and for students, is to assess the implications of these underlying changes for the forms of the international system; both in their effect on states' freedom of action, perhaps even on their viability as independent political entities, and in their implications for the future development of the system.

Part of the problem is to discern what sort of effect these continuing changes are likely to have on the nation-state and the international system, and to predict whether we are still in a period of rapid change or are at last reaching a stable plateau. Looking at some indicators, the system appears in balance. 'The world distribution of power has been more stable since 1945 than at any time since the 1890s. Other developments since 1945 [for instance, the development of nuclear weapons, creating a new balance of "absolute power"] have, moreover, made the present stability more solid than that of earlier times.'[38] Looking at the end of European dominance and the great upheaval of decolonisation, it seems that 'the present period marks with unusual clarity the end of an era in world affairs'.[39] Looking at the implications of the technological and political changes which have taken place since 1945, on the other hand, the present outlook and habits of interaction of states appear to lag behind the requirements of the international system.[40] Looking ahead in the light of 'the necessities of economic and technological progress', it seems unlikely that the nation-state will be able to cope with the pressure of internal demands and external problems without evolving new and more intimate forms of international co-operation.[41]

The impact of these changes on the position of the nation-state is far from clear. Certainly, most writers are agreed, it has reduced the ability of the major powers to impose their will on the international system; 'the weight of the power of most governments, and particularly of the great powers, has been declining ever since 1945'.[42] One widely received view some years ago held that, with continuing trends in economic inter-dependence, cross-national ideologies and means of warfare, 'whatever remained of the impermeability of states seems to have gone for good'; but its author has recently revised his conclusion that states as the central units of international politics were in decline to take into account the continuing resilience of nationalism and national independence.[43] In the early years of the development of European integration some influential academic writers saw the process of community formation as almost self-advancing, spilling over from one functional area to another;[44] and this belief in a trend towards integration was easily transferred to other international regions. In the disillusioned situation of the late sixties, observers were more struck by evidence of 'national self-preoccupation', re-examining trend patterns to discover that societies were growing more inward-looking and the world less interdependent.[45]

Students and policy-makers are also uncertain about the implications of these changes for the conduct and the coverage of foreign policy. The development of new and more personal styles of diplomacy, of new forums for political interaction in international organisations and conferences, is generally noted, as is the extension of the area of political relations from its nineteenth-century boundaries to cover science and technology, monetary policy, transport regulation, cultural policy and even sport; but opinions are divided on how welcome these developments are, and how far states should adjust to them.[46] To the more conservative, a return to traditional diplomacy, based on a clear conception of differing national interests, is indicated.[47] To the more radical, 'the logic of the argument that the European nation-state is for many purposes obsolescent is unanswerable', and policy-makers should adjust their working practices to meet the need for continuous multilateral co-operation and to fit in to new institutions.[48] Against the traditionalist view of foreign policy as essentially diplomacy, one government report accepts that external relations 'involve us in contacts over a much wider range of government and society than has been usual in traditional diplomacy, and that these contacts are concerned with many topics which have in the past been conventionally regarded as belonging to the domestic affairs of sovereign states'.[49]

The external environment, then, does not provide the policy-maker with any clear or self-evident indication of the best or most rational direction to take. The 'facts of international life' are those perceived by the policy-maker; not any objective or constant reality, but the world as he and his advisers see it.

3 Policy-making

States do not make policy: governments do. In foreign policy, as in domestic policy, they make their plans and take their decisions under pressure from a number of different sources. The international environment exerts a constant and restraining pressure, as we have seen. The process of domestic politics, arguably, exerts a similar restraint. The pressure of events and of the flow of incoming information, the ever-present pressure of time, and the limitations imposed by the structure of government all crowd in on the policy-maker.

There are now some 140 states in the international system, interacting politically over a wide and expanding range of areas, both bilaterally and through a large number of multilateral international organisations. The mass of relevant information, the number of relevant events which policy-makers need to be aware of, is enormous. The British Foreign and Commonwealth Office receives some 2000 telegrams and dispatches from its missions abroad each day; in addition information, and requests for information or decisions, flow in from other government ministries, intelligence reports are received from the government's intelligence apparatus, while the 134 foreign missions in London and the officials of international organisations send in their own reports and requests. The most immediate problem confronting the foreign policy-maker is to absorb and reduce to order the material which faces him.[50]

The international system is not only complex. It is also in continuous movement. Crises threaten, and must be dealt with before they blow up to serious proportions; opportunities arise, and must be taken before they are lost; negotiations proceed, and must be attended to before they break down. The pressure for output, for decisions to be made and instructions given, is therefore as heavy as the inward flow of information. Yet, while subordinate officials may be able to devote their whole attention to these problems, senior policy-makers can give only part of their time to the problems of policy. They are, after all, actors not only in the international system but also in domestic politics; the cultivation and protection of their domestic base, from which they derive their political authority, must often take first priority. The expansion of the international system, the growth of international travel and of personal diplomacy, have added to the burdens on their time. Attending international conferences, receiving and entertaining the growing procession of visiting foreign dignitaries, the time-consuming civilities of diplomatic discourse as well as the useful exchange of political ideas, all eat into the time available for deciding policy. 'No democratic system yet devised has even attempted to solve the problem of the crushing responsibility borne by foreign ministers.'[51] Senior policy-makers in non-democratic states, where policy is seldom so well divided into separate areas through a stable decision-making structure, must find the burden even more crushing, the demands on their attention even more distracting.

In all states, to a greater or a lesser degree, foreign policy emerges out of an institutional process. In developed states, it is extremely rare for foreign policy decisions to be the responsibility of a single individual, or a small group. The need for information, interpretation and advice, and the necessity of co-ordinating policies between different areas and different ministries, involve a large number of men and agencies in the evolution of policy. Foreign policy is made within an organisational context, which consists of the foreign ministry itself, the various government intelligence agencies, those other ministerial departments involved (which will include at a minimum those departments responsible for defence, foreign trade and external financial relations), and the machinery for central co-ordination and decision, be it Politburo, Cabinet or White House.[52] The effort to ensure continuity and coherence requires regular procedures for internal co-ordination, institutionalised in a series of committees, in carefully maintained records, and in the constant circulation of files and position papers; the effect of these procedures on policy is, inevitably, to create 'a certain inertia in the system'.[53] The internal structure of this institutional process, the pattern of consultation and decision, the availability and circulation of (often confidential) information, have a direct effect upon the content of the policies which emerge, and as such have been the concern of successive policy-makers through successive reorganisations of its structure, and the focus of regular academic criticism.[54]

The foreign policy-making process therefore displays a number of necessary, if not ideal, characteristics. The pressure of immediacy accounts for one commonly observed, and as frequently criticised, characteristic: that 'energy and thought tend to be concentrated on the immediate, rather than on the fundamental'.[55] The limitations of time and of competing concerns for the policy-makers' attention account for the tendency to maintain existing policies, or to make only incremental rather than major changes in the direction of policy. 'Any policy that is relatively easy to discover, that fits in well with the previously established thought habits of the relevant decision-makers, and that has no obvious major drawbacks, has a good chance to be adopted.'[56] The number of different problems and crises demanding the policy-makers' attention forces even the largest organisation to concentrate on those which they consider most urgent, to select the problems which appear most important, to the neglect of others. 'The burden of simultaneous responses to external demands may be a crucial determinant in the timing of actions and the nature or amount of policy-making resources which are devoted to specific actions.'[57] In a crisis situation the upper echelons of the policy-making structure may be almost completely preoccupied with the load of incoming messages and outgoing instructions generated by a single problem, and so unable to cope with any but routine decisions on other questions.[58]

The policy-maker, then, is unable to absorb the universe of international transactions which faces him. He must have some criterion for selecting out of the mass of incoming information what is most relevant to his concerns. But information in itself is of little use to him without interpretation. A report may be received, for example, about the number of Russian naval vessels in the Indian Ocean. In order to assess the relevance of this information to policy, and to determine what reaction (if any) is called for, the policy-maker needs, first, to refer to earlier reports on the subject, to trace (if he can) the pattern behind the single event; secondly, to place this pattern of behaviour within his general understanding of Soviet foreign policy, to assess what motive lies behind it, what are the likely Soviet objectives; thirdly, to consider his state's own interests and objectives in the Indian Ocean; and fourthly, to decide how seriously and in what manner (if at all) those interests are affected by Soviet moves. The same report is therefore likely to receive a different priority, and to evoke a different response, in different governments. The governments of India, Britain, the United States and Kenya may all consider the report significant, and will interpret it in the light of their different interests and understandings of Soviet intentions; the government of Canada may consider it unimportant in the light of its own interests and concerns.

Foreign policy-making takes place, therefore, within a conceptual as well as an organisational framework, which serves to simplify the complexities of the situation, and to guide the government's response. Such frameworks are characteristic of the pattern of domestic policy-making as much as of foreign policy;[59] but in foreign policy the greater mass of information, the greater complexity of the system, and the greater degree of unfamiliarity with the behaviour and the background of other actors which confront the policy-maker, all make reliance on such conceptual frameworks more essential. The elements of such a framework, it may be suggested, will include the following: a view of the decisive determinants of international behaviour, which will guide the degree of significance the policy-maker gives to other governments' public pronouncements, their domestic circumstances, their economic and commercial policy, their geographical situation and their military dispositions;[60] a set of views on the foreign policy attitudes of other powers, and of the main constraints which operate upon them, which will guide his interpretation of their actions, and his assessment of the correct response;[61] a view of his state's position in the world, its distinctive 'role' and its rightful status; a set of views on his state's 'national interest', on its interests abroad and its foreign policy objectives; and an assessment of the resources at his disposal. For some policy-makers this overall framework, this set of guiding generalisations about their environment, may be largely conscious and explicit.[62] For most, too preoccupied with policy for contemplation or self-examination, it serves as an implicit foundation for their 'practical' concerns.

The policy-maker's assessment of his available resources, it may be noted, is also partly subjective and conceptual – based partly on his knowledge of the domestic capabilities, in trained personnel, military forces (actual and potential), funds and productive capacity, at his disposal, and partly on his perception of what kinds of resources are available for political use.[63] To the French government under President de Gaulle monetary reserves were a resource for directly political use; to the Soviet government cultural exchanges and trading agreements; to the African countries sporting relations. Yet other governments have not seen these to be political resources, or have considered their use improper or illegitimate. The policy-maker's assessment of what is political in international relations, of what transactions are relevant to foreign policy and in what way, is similarly subjective. The British government, for instance, has held trade with Cuba and South Africa to be matters of private commercial concern, while the governments of the United States and the African Commonwealth see them as fit subjects for political protest.

The academic student is also in need of a framework with which to comprehend, order and explain the relationship between the policy-maker and his environment. In this he has not yet been well served; partly because the focus of such a framework lies directly across the boundary between the two academic disciplines (with foreign policy as an area of study too often left to the students of international politics alone), partly because the weight of secrecy and security which shrouds the area discourages attempts at study. Snyder, Bruck and Sapin's ambitious and comprehensive conceptualisation of foreign policy-making 'as decision-making in an organisational context', originally published in 1954, has been widely cited and frequently reprinted.[64] Its emphasis on the psychological and subjective aspects of policy-making, the importance of perception and interpretation, its characterisation of the external environment as 'composed of what the decision-makers decide is important',[65] have been widely influential; but its very comprehensiveness and complexity have proved a handicap to further development and application.[66] A useful and stimulating, if necessarily loose, model of the decision-making process is provided by Joseph Frankel in *The Making of Foreign Policy*, conceptualising decision-makers as 'individuals who arrive at their decisions by confronting their values with their image of the environment'.[67]

There are, however, difficulties in conceptualising foreign policy-making as a series of finite decisions. To abstract a particular decision out of the continuous process of routine decisions and non-decisions is to distort the process, to underplay 'the continuous stream of activities in which decisions are embedded', and to overemphasise the 'big' decisions.[68] Only in a situation of crisis is the build-up to a major decision easily recognisable; 'many important decisions', critics have argued, 'are only detectable as such after the event'.[69] It is more useful, and more accurate, to conceptualise policy-making as a flow of policy, a continuing interchange of information and instructions between the policy-making organisation and its environment.[70] For this Karl Deutsch's work on communications theory has provided a number of valuable concepts, of 'message', 'reception', 'feedback' and 'steering'.[71] Much of the literature on domestic policy-making – the work of Lindblom, Herbert Simon and others on decision-making and organisation, for instance – has also proved valuable, generating concepts which have by now been absorbed into the foreign policy literature.[72] But we do not yet have an agreed overall framework for the foreign policy field, detailed enough to cover its main characteristics but straightforward enough to be easily applied, which can serve as a foundation for future study. In this respect, it is still fair to say, the study of foreign policy 'is devoid of general theory'.[73]

The concentration of academic study in this area has been on the conceptual rather than on the organisational context of policy-making: on policy-makers' images of the world and of their country's place in the world, on their images of other states' attitudes, on the nature and definition of the objectives which they pursue. The language of foreign policy-making is full of references to objectives: to 'national purposes', to 'vital interests', to 'goals', above all to the 'national interest'. Students and critics alike have therefore been drawn to examine these objectives; to determine, if they can, the values which underlie them, or the degree to which objectives are 'realistic' in terms of a state's resources or its international environment.

The concept of national interest has had an enduring appeal both for politicians and for academic critics. For politicians it has served both to legitimise their external objectives and to cut short domestic debate about those objectives. To say that an action is 'in the national interest' is to label those who oppose it as disloyal, and to identify the government's action with values and symbols above party politics. For critics it appeared to offer an objective standard by which to assess the wisdom or unwisdom of statesmen's conduct of foreign policy. Thus Hans Morgenthau, Walter Lippmann and others concerned with the failure of the Western democracies to avoid the Second World War, identified the cause of the failure in their policy-makers' neglect of their national interest in favour of mistaken conceptions of international morality or misconceived respect for domestic public opinion. The failure had been, they concluded, in the incapacity of democratic governments 'to cope with reality, to govern their affairs, to defend their vital interests';[74] the remedy lay in a proper awareness of the nature of their country's national interest, and in its steady pursuit. The concept of national interest, then, implies the existence of a set of stable, relatively unchanging foreign policy goals, recognisable and identifiable alike to the enlightened statesman and the rational observer.[75] The reader will recognise the link between this concept and the idea of bipartisanship in foreign policy – and with those approaches which see foreign policy as characterised by its stability and continuity over time, or as largely determined by the international environment.

The problem is to identify and to define the national interest. For Morgenthau, 'political realism' is to be found in 'the concept of interest defined in terms of power'.[76] The national interest, that is, is assumed to lie in the husbanding and the furtherance of national power. But this takes us little further, for 'power' is itself an imprecise concept. 'In practice power is not merely a goal but is also a means to an end'; pursued and husbanded, it may be argued, not for itself but as the most important means available for the furtherance of other goals.[77]

The most fundamental of these goals, we may agree, are national survival and national security – the protection and preservation of the political system as such; but it is hard to argue that these are the only observable goals.[78] Most governments pursue economic goals as a major foreign policy objective: the pursuit of trading advantages, the advancement and protection of foreign investment, the acquisition of materials, equipment and technological information for their domestic economy. Governments have pursued international status, prestige, 'grandeur' in itself as a goal of foreign policy, and have expended considerable resources in its pursuit.[79] The goals at stake in foreign policy may even be domestic objectives: the preservation of the existing social structure (seen to be at stake in Italian foreign policy) or the maintenance of the regime itself.[80] If these are all to be subsumed under the concept of national interest, then the term is too all-embracing to be useful; if, as the political realists wish, they are to be arranged into a clear hierarchy according to objective and rational criteria, then these criteria are not self-evident.[81]

A clear and agreed definition of national interest, then, would require agreement as to the nature and priority of the values which objectives ought to express, and would have to assume rationality on the part of the policy-maker and of the academic observer. But this raises the whole question of rationality in foreign policy. We have already noted the complex of pressures, in terms of time, inadequate information, simultaneity of problems, and stress, which limit the policy-maker's alternatives and force him to take decisions in situations of uncertainty. Even if the institutional process has attained a high standard of instrumental rationality, in its collection and assimilation of information, in its capacity to handle a number of problems quickly and in parallel, the policy-maker is still left with a crucial area of uncertainty. The problem must first be clearly identified and defined – that is, set within a perceptual framework which relates it to other problems and to the government's main concerns. This is, except in times of crisis, most often a routine matter, fitting new information into accepted frameworks; but there is a good deal of ambiguity in most international situations, sufficient to make more than one interpretation plausible. An efficient foreign policy organisation may be able to cope appropriately and immediately with a foreign threat; the difficulty is to determine whether a particular movement of troops, a particular act of discrimination against one's foreign trade, does or does not present a threat, and if so to assess what level of threat it presents. The policy-maker must then determine which of his state's interests are most affected, and which goals are most important in determining his response. For this he needs, not general long-term objectives, but immediate operational goals; he needs to know, further, what weight he should give to competing goals in a specific situation. Faced with an E.E.C. levy on chicken imports, for instance, it is of little immediate help to an American policy-maker to know that freer international trade is in his country's national interest. It is more directly helpful to know how his government sees the development and strengthening of the E.E.C. as fitting in with this long-term objective, and how much weight he should give to this goal as against such goals as strengthening the United States balance of payments or protecting the interests of American farmers. For this he needs to know his own, and his superiors', values: the strength of their belief in the desirability of international co-operation, the weight they attach to promoting the interests of particular domestic groups, and so on.[82]

The problem of rationality is much more acute in assessing the motives and likely behaviour of other states' policy-makers. In domestic politics policy-makers operate on the basis of shared values, of an underlying consensus on the objectives which the government ought to promote and the limitations on its permissible range of actions. It is easy to assume that a similar consensus exists in other countries, resting on similar values. Such an assumption lay behind the optimistic belief in the power of world opinion which many Western policy-makers and academics held between the wars; and such a simplifying assumption lies behind the realists' assertion that all states seek power or national security. Observably, the values which political systems attach to particular objectives – to the preservation of life, the protection of minorities, the institution of private property, the importance of prestige, the survival of the state as such – differ according to their differing cultures; and the differing weights attached by each political system to each value will clearly affect the direction of their foreign policies.[83] A more fundamental difficulty than this, given the diversity of cultures now included within the global international system, is the possibility that other states may have a different conception of rationality from our own: that the cultural relativity of values is matched by 'the cultural relativity of the processes of mind'.[84] What is rational behaviour for an American in a given situation may, therefore, not be rational for a Chinese or a Vietnamese.[85]

The idea of an objective national interest, common to all states or peculiar to one, must, therefore, be rejected. It is an attractive concept: it represents the longing for certainty and clarity in foreign policy, in place of the uncertainty and confusion which characterise the field. But states are not single-purpose organisations; and not even the academic observer, equipped through hindsight with a broader view than that available to the policy-maker, can claim complete objectivity.[86] His criticism of the conduct of policy is affected by his ranking of the values which policy-makers ought to have obeyed; 'we evaluate as we breathe', and our value preferences are reflected in our interpretation of events.[87] This does not mean, however, that we are unable to discuss, classify and criticise the several and conflicting foreign policy objectives which governments pursue in a meaningful and useful fashion.

The distinction between long-term objectives and short-term operational goals – or, as Arnold Wolfers labels them, 'aspirations' and 'policy goals' – has already been noted.[88] The relationship between these immediate and long-term objectives is complex. Policy goals may be seen as operationalising aspirations in specific situations. Success in achieving policy goals may encourage the development of new aspirations, and prolonged failure may lead to the abandonment of both goals and the aspirations which lie behind them. Not all a state's expressed foreign policy aspirations may be formulated into immediate goals – the international situation may be seen to be inhospitable to their immediate fulfilment, or the significance attached to them may be more symbolic than practical. Thus the members of the North Atlantic Alliance have agreed since its formation on the reunification of Germany as a long-term objective, but for most of the last twenty years have had no immediate proposals for its achievement.[89]

Wolfers distinguishes further between sets of contrasting, and often conflicting, foreign policy goals.[90] He distinguishes between 'possession goals' and 'milieu goals': the former relating to direct national advantage – tariff concessions, territorial gains, extra-territorial privileges – at the cost of other states, the latter to shaping the conditions of the international environment – freedom of the seas, respect for international law, a stable international monetary system. A similar distinction is often made, at a less sophisticated level, between 'enlightened' and 'narrow' national interests. He distinguishes 'direct national goals', which benefit the state as a whole – national independence, national security or national welfare – from those 'indirect national goals' which benefit particular groups, whether private interests in democratic countries or particular élite groups in non-democratic countries.[91] And he distinguishes, and contrasts, 'ideological or revolutionary goals', universalist commitments to make the world safe for democracy or to forward the world Communist revolution, and 'traditional national goals', more conservative, directly national concerns.

This last distinction is close to one made in many critical studies of foreign policy, between 'myth' and 'reality'. Senator Fulbright has characterised the predicament of American foreign policy in terms of the gap between 'old myths and new realities'.[92] Post-war French foreign policy has been described as shaped by nineteenth-century 'dogmas and myths that were ultimately separated from twentieth-century reality'; British foreign policy as spellbound by 'illusions' of the past.[93] The objectives of a country's foreign policy and the conceptual frameworks which surround them, these critics argue, can be judged by how closely they fit the realities and the possibilities of the international situation. This is perhaps too simple a judgment: it overestimates the degree to which any policy-maker or observer can ever be sure what the reality of any situation is, and underestimates the role of myth in shaping that reality. The myth of French greatness was, for a while, a real resource for de Gaulle's foreign policy; just as the myth of Britain's great power status gave Britain additional international influence, until shattered by the country's chronic economic weakness. But it does point to two further frequently made criticisms of foreign policy objectives: the need to define, and to redefine, a country's main objectives, and the need to maintain a balance between goals and resources.[94]

Britain's lack of clearly defined and understood objectives, her 'piecemeal' and 'pragmatic' approach to foreign policy, has been blamed by many commentators for what they see as the failure of her policies since the Second World War.[95] The lack of any ' "great debate" for the purpose of redefining the French position and status in the world' has been seen as accounting for the weakness of the Fourth Republic's foreign policy.[96] The problem is that objectives tend to persist: 'vital' interests are pursued long after they have ceased to be either vital or attainable, partly because of the sheer inertia of accepted beliefs, partly because the goals of foreign policy are so easily identified with fundamental national aims, and so placed above criticism.[97] The need is for objectives to be made explicit; for their relevance and consistency to be regularly re-examined; and for governments to match their objectives to their available resources. Examination of this last relationship has also concentrated on Britain and France, as over-extended countries whose commitments have considerably exceeded their resources, though it could as fruitfully focus on West Germany or Japan, as states with 'spare 'resources as yet uncommitted. Clearly the relationship between these is not invariable; the balance between resources devoted to domestic purposes and those devoted to foreign is a variable factor, depending on the balance of social values between domestic and foreign objectives. But it may be argued that there is a long-term tendency for objectives and commitments to balance, for the one to adjust to the other.

The impetus behind a good deal of recent theoretical work in the fields of international politics and foreign policy has been the aim of assisting the policy-maker: in defining his objectives, communicating them to other states' policy-makers, and choosing the most rational means of attaining them, in more clearly assessing the outlines of the international situation and predicting its most likely future direction. The work of Karl Deutsch and his school on communications theory has been concerned not only with refining the definition of concepts, but also with providing new insights for the policy-maker on the importance of information and information processing, on the role of perception, and on the nature and significance of the exchange of communications between different states.[98] The communications approach has also been concerned with the identification and collection of quantifiable data on international transactions, to assist the student and the policy-maker to monitor change and stability in the international system.[99] The theory of games has been used by a number of theorists to study, in 'laboratory' situations, the reaction of 'decision-makers' to bargaining situations and the pattern of choice particular situations generate, with the aim of enlightening policy-makers as to the choices available to them and the likely reactions of their opponents.[100] The use of gaming, developed out of nineteenth-century war-gaming into a sophisticated technique for 'playing' international situations, and of simulated models of the international system, made possible by the development of the computer and the assembly of quantifiable data on international transactions, is attracting growing attention in academic and government circles in a number of countries.[101]

There are a good many problems involved in the use of these new techniques for research or policy-planning. The most serious is the inability of game theory and simulation to cope with non-rational aspects of foreign policy-making: values, emotions, perception, the impact of personality. Game theory, for instance, 'requires that each player himself should have a set of consistent policy objectives', and that 'each player should choose his strategies consistent with the expectations he can rationally entertain about other players' behaviour'.[102] Almost as serious is the difficulty of quantifying much of the most relevant data, and the doubtful basis on which weights must be assigned to the different categories of data. To an extent these problems are avoided in gaming, by the use of teams of players to represent the human factor; but there remains the problem of a game's replicability under 'real' conditions with 'real' policy-makers, which throws doubt on the possibilities of prediction.

There remains a good deal of academic scepticism, as well

as academic enthusiasm, about the usefulness of these techniques. So far only the American government has invested significant resources in their development, or applied their concepts and insights to policy-making to any degree – with results that are still mixed and uncertain.[103] Their proponents would argue that these techniques are still at an early stage of development, and that their potential is far greater than their limited achievement so far. Within the academic discipline of international relations they have proved a prolific source of concepts, a strong pressure towards the careful construction of theoretical frameworks, and a useful aid to teaching. For the policy-maker they offer assistance in training, and arguably a valuable aid to policy planning: 'prediction does not have to be right to be instructive', provided its conclusions are cautiously used.[104] The problems governments face in absorbing and interpreting the mass of information which they need to know about changing conditions in the international environment, and the consequent attraction of improving their ability to handle it and their flexibility in understanding it, of reducing the area of uncertainty, ensure that they will attract growing interest, not only from academics, but from policy-makers themselves.[105]

4 The Domestic Process

In the nineteenth-century international system the domestic context of foreign policy could to a considerable degree be taken as given. Only in the short and intermittent wars were the mass of the population involved to any degree in bearing the burdens of external affairs. Few of the major states were democracies; those that were, with few exceptions, carefully excluded foreign policy questions from the democratic sphere. The international economy was developing, but as yet involved in most countries only a minority of commercial interests and a small minority of the working population. Gladstone might stump the country, electioneering on the Bulgarian atrocities. In the United States, the great exception, newspaper sensationalism and public opinion might evoke the Spanish–American War. But on the whole the world of diplomacy remained an intimate and aristocratic one, in which Sir Edward Grey might sanction conversations with the French, or even send the fateful ultimatum to Germany, without consulting the Cabinet,[106] in which the Queen of England might begin a letter to the Emperor of Germany: 'As Your Grandmother to whom you have always shown so much affection . . . I feel I cannot refrain from expressing my deep regret at the telegram you sent President Kruger',[107] and in which most diplomats shared a common language, a common culture and a common loyalty to the international system which set them apart from their domestic environment. Foreign policy, very clearly, was a matter for the executive branch of government.

Yet even before 1914 the international and domestic conditions which supported this aristocratic insulation of foreign policy from domestic politics had been considerably undermined. Since then the transformation of the environment of foreign policy by political, economic, technological and social developments has entirely altered the policy-makers' situation.

The changes in the international environment have been discussed above. The expansion of government concerns, in social welfare, education, domestic economic policy, transport policy, and so on, has brought their populations into far closer contact with the business of national government. Mass education, and mass literacy, have widened the potential circle of informed public opinion; radio and television, arguably, have widened it still further. The increased demands which external policy (above all in the shape of defence policy) now make on domestic resources, the sharper competition for resources between different sectors in countries committed to economic growth and social improvement, and the impact which the high level of government spending makes on citizens in the form of taxes, have brought the pressure of foreign policy to bear much more directly in domestic politics.[108] Conscription in two long world wars, and in many states in peace-time, has involved citizens even more directly in the consequences of their governments' foreign policies. The expansion of international trade, and the revolution in communications, with its effects on travel and cross-national contact, have considerably increased the proportion of citizens with a degree of personal involvement or personal experience in extra-national relations.

It would seem incontrovertible, then, that 'foreign policy, like all politics, can no longer be made by the few'.[109] Yet most academic observers are still agreed that, for most purposes, 'foreign policy is made and opinion is shaped by a very small group of persons'.[110] The conventional wisdom of academic interpretation, it would be fair to say, remains that foreign policy is an élite process, dominated by the executive, in all developed states; though one professor who moved across to making policy admitted his 'recognition of the powerful place of domestic politics in the formulation of foreign policies' as his first impression of the different perspective he gained inside government.[111] The degree to which foreign policy has remained a separate area, or has become part of the domestic political process, is therefore a matter of some uncertainty.

Unfortunately this is also a neglected area of political study. Many texts on international politics relegate consideration of the non-executive aspects of domestic politics to a single chapter on 'the domestic environment'. Studies of domestic politics more often deal with the substance of foreign policy than the process. 'Foreign policy phenomena', one writer concludes, 'are the unwanted stepchildren of political systems',[112] assumed by both disciplines and properly studied by neither. The literature that we have consists primarily of single-country studies, and that available in English covers the major countries very unevenly. Not surprisingly, the United States is the most fully researched; indeed, the literature on American foreign policy so far outweighs the rest of the field. In attempting to generalise about the nature of the foreign policy process, one is open to objections that the internal or external situation of each country is unique: the United States because of the exceptional character of her domestic politics, West Germany because of her peculiar international predicament, the Soviet Union because of the absence of democratic politics and her position as the mentor of the Communist world. There are, however, a number of common features worth further comparative examination. Looked at as an aspect of domestic politics, foreign policy may usefully be seen as an 'issue area' characterised in developed states, like other issue areas, by a distinctive set of values at stake and by distinctive institutions, actors, and roles.[113] To explore the domestic foreign policy process within this framework (which is indeed almost the only framework provided by the literature) may help to illuminate its domestic significance.

The values at stake in foreign policy, as we have seen, are distinguished by their close connection with the symbols of the state: security, national standing, sovereignty, territorial integrity. These set foreign policy apart from, even above, domestic politics; yet there are a number of other values at stake which are more closely linked to the distinctive issues of domestic politics. The demands made by external policy upon resources, in the form of defence expenditure and the manpower and production needed to support defence, foreign aid, and expenditure across the balance of payments, are in direct competition with other calls upon a state's scarce resources, for personal consumption, social expenditure and capital investment. To question the need for a given level of defence spending must be to question the nature of the external threat or the extent of a state's foreign commitments; so that to argue for higher chemical investment in the Soviet Union involves arguing for a 'softer' policy towards the West, and to argue for new federal spending in American cities involves questioning the priority of the Vietnam war.[114] The proportion of a state's resources and manpower involved in the defence sector creates its own, powerful interest, defending and furthering its own values: the 'military-industrial complex' has been distinguished as a major factor in domestic politics in several countries.[115] The status of these and other groups may be at issue in a country's foreign policy – the status of the Soviet military, at risk in a period of relaxed tension,[116] or the comparative status of the American Negro population and the southern whites, at stake in United States policy towards Africa.[117] 'The principal issue in Italian foreign policy is whether to preserve or change the domestic social structure';[118] at stake as much in Italy's foreign alignments as in the domestic struggle between Christian Democrats and Communists. More than this, the very status and legitimacy of a regime may be at stake in its foreign policy. In the Soviet Union, Stalin's foreign policy was viewed 'through the prism of internal needs and problems, principally that of maintaining the dictator's rule unchanged'; while post-Stalin foreign policy is limited in its ability to revise its external aims by the link between its ideological commitment (and the presence of external 'enemies') and its internal legitimacy.[119]

Foreign policy issues clearly act as a resource in the domestic political process in many countries. In the Soviet Union they provide a powerful resource in the factional struggle among the top leadership.[120] In countries with ethnic minorities, foreign policy questions may be an important electoral resource – the expellees in post-war Germany,[121] the Jews and other 'hyphenated Americans' in the United States. Images of the outside world are also a resource for domestic politics. Politicians all too frequently assume the mantle of international statesmanship, or claim credit for their country's international standing, to strengthen their appeal to the voters or their prestige among their colleagues. The flow of foreign visitors to Washington, to be photographed in earnest conversation with the President, and the 'world tours' which are almost obligatory for American presidential contenders, testify to the perceived effectiveness of this resource. The image of an external threat, real or imagined, is a powerful means of promoting national unity, or building a sense of nationhood.[122] Where a clear threat is lacking, the exaggeration of a potential threat or even the creation of an imaginary one has often served to strengthen popular support for a regime, or as the pretext for suppressing domestic opposition.[123] In spite of its links with the symbols of statehood – or on occasion because of them – foreign policy has not infrequently been a major divisive issue in domestic politics: dividing the parties over the country's fundamental orientation in post-war West Germany (a state effectively shaped by its foreign policy) and Japan, splitting the Italian Socialists in 1947 and the Japanese Socialists in 1959, a major issue in successive American presidential elections.[124] The separability of foreign policy issues from domestic politics must therefore be seen as relative and variable.

More has been written on the subject of public opinion and foreign policy than on any other domestic aspect of the field. The 'invasion' of the foreign policy area by enthusiasts for democratic control in the wake of the First World War, the outbreak of which many blamed on the undemocratic and élitist nature of pre-war diplomacy, introduced a major new element into foreign policy-making in Britain.[125] 'Prior to the First World War public opinion usually had a negligible influence on British foreign policy, which remained the prerogative of a political élite. After the First World War no politician could afford to overlook the enthusiasms of the electorate, however ill-informed he might consider it to be.'[126] In the United States, public opinion had become a major factor in foreign policy well before 1914, and had done much to precipitate the war with Spain;[127] between the wars domestic attitudes, forcefully expressed by Congressional leaders, were a very powerful influence on American foreign and defence policy. The Second World War brought a strong reaction. The weakness and inadequacy of the democracies' diplomacy was attributed to their leaders' willingness to follow public opinion rather than to lead it.[128] The uninformed nature of mass opinion on foreign policy was stressed, as well as its fickleness. Out of this reaction came both the call for a return to a more 'traditional' style of policy, and a number of academic studies of the role of public opinion in this field.[129]

Since the Second World War the accumulation of opinion poll data, and the stimulus provided by the United States government's interest in maintaining public support for its foreign policies at home and abroad, have encouraged continued academic study.[130] 'After thirty years of public opinion research, the data on public attitudes to foreign policy questions have reached mountainous proportions and have formed the basis for many studies'; and the common conclusion shows 'the large majority of the population to be uninterested and uninformed on foreign policy'.[131] For the mass of the population foreign policy issues are remote considerations, on which they feel a low sense of subjective competence, and are therefore content, for most purposes, to leave responsibility to those with a degree of expertise or specialised influence, and to hold them responsible if they experience any direct adverse effects.[132] In foreign policy the relevant public is not the mass public but the 'attentive public', that 'small stratum of the public' whose occupational responsibilities require them to pay attention to the international scene, or whose self-image of their role and interests leads them to feel involved in foreign affairs.[133] The degree of their interest and involvement does not extend evenly over the whole foreign policy area. The businessman involved in international commerce, the campaigner for human rights, the schoolteacher teaching 'world affairs', will focus on concerns which overlap only rarely. Foreign policy has not one but several involved publics: 'one "attentive public" for agricultural policy, another for Latin American affairs, and perhaps still another for policy towards Asia'.[134]

The foreign policy issue area, then, draws upon only a very limited and specialised public for domestic interest and for continued and positive involvement. But in a wider sense mass public opinion acts as a strong negative constraint on the making of foreign policy. It 'sets the outer limits beyond which policy choices cannot be made'.[135] Particularly in democratic states, it provides a strong force for continuity in foreign policy, in the support which the public gives for traditional goals or established interests,[136] and in the potential for rapid increases in public involvement in opposition to new policy departures the development of which the public has not followed and the reasons for which the public does not understand. The development of public opinion polling has made policy-makers more aware of mass opinion, and so has strengthened this constraint – though the knowledge that elections in democratic states 'are not won primarily on the basis of issues, particularly issues of foreign policy', leaves the policy-maker considerable flexibility in following, or ignoring, or trying to change public attitudes.[137] It is partly because foreign policy questions are generally of low salience that public attitudes are so resistant to change – and that it requires such positive efforts on the part of political leaders to mould public opinion on foreign policy questions, to create and maintain support for policies which appear remote or threatening to the public at large. This task of cultivating domestic support, academic writers agree, should be one of the first concerns of foreign policy-makers.[138] A further problem is that mass opinion, when finally aroused by politicians' propaganda or the stress of crisis, is an unstable and unsettling force: a source of positive feedback when statesmen try to damp down the emotions they have aroused, a source of internal disorder and discontent under prolonged strain.[139]

The policy-maker in this area, then, must address himself to different audiences: to those foreign governments who are his fellow-participants in the process of international politics (and to their domestic publics), and to his own political base in his domestic public. It is not easy to please all at once; there is, therefore, a frequent temptation to say different things to one's domestic audience from what is said abroad, or to use language to evoke support in one audience which is likely to alarm or offend the other. 'To mobilise support for policies, Americans say things to themselves that from the standpoint of other peoples might better be left unsaid.'[140] In this respect non-democratic states have at least as large a problem as democratic countries; the more rumbustious language customarily used to arouse mass support and to castigate 'enemies of the people' or 'enemies of the state' fits even less easily with the language of diplomatic persuasion.

Far less has been written on the role or effectiveness of organised groups in the foreign policy process. The general conclusion of most studies is that 'group organisation and articulation is relatively weak in foreign policy matters', and their influence correspondingly less than on domestic issues;[141] but this is more often asserted than documented. Organised attempts to influence foreign policy are not a new phenomenon. In Britain the anti-Slavery groups, which began in the late eighteenth century, and the Anti-Corn Law League were among the earliest successful promotional organisations.[142] The 'China lobby' in American politics, the 'Katanga lobby' in British, and many others in these and other states, have been credited or blamed for influencing their governments' policies. As wide a spread of groups exists in the foreign policy area as in the domestic: from campaigning organisations promoting peace, aid or international understanding, to ethnic or religious groups representing moral or cultural interests and business groups representing economic interests. Their recruitment is limited by the smallness of the attentive public for foreign policy; their ability to influence the government is limited by the pressures of the international environment. Academic attempts to assess the extent of their influence are limited by the peculiar secrecy which surrounds the foreign policy process in most countries. 'There is very widespread agreement that the most influential interest groups in the foreign policy field, as in the domestic arena, are economic interest groups – business organisations, trade associations, and the like'; though 'the evidence to back up these generalisations is not abundant'.[143] In other areas of foreign policy there is general agreement that 'interest group influence on foreign policy is slight';[144] though here again the evidence to support this statement is scanty. The need for more research in this area is apparent.[145]

One peculiarity of group activity in the foreign policy area is that, for some purposes, foreign governments and foreign groups act, directly or indirectly, overtly or covertly, as groups in the domestic process. 'The great majority of the societies for promoting good relations between the United Kingdom and another country receive aid in cash or kind from the Government of the latter, though the amounts involved are usually only a few hundred pounds or less'.[146] 'Foreign groups are not only interested in American policy, they also can have a significant influence upon it.'[147] This penetration of the domestic policy process by foreign actors casts some doubts on the separability of the internal aspects of foreign policy from the international, which will be explored further in the final section.

Discussion of the involvement of groups in the foreign policy process merges into discussion of the foreign policy élite. The wider élite, in most countries, consists partly of the leading representatives of non-official and official organisations: the military, for instance, a highly 'interested' section of the élite, or the leaders of the commercial and financial community. As with the attentive publics for foreign policy issues, the relevant élites are a small and specialised stratum of national élite groups. For the majority of civil servants, business leaders, politicians, journalists and publicists, the domestic arena is a far more direct and pressing concern. Only those whose specific interests or responsibilities involve them in external affairs are likely to devote time to keeping informed on foreign policy issues, or to expend much effort on trying to influence the government's position on them. 'Hence the pattern of leadership activity in the foreign area will ordinarily be substantially more concentrated than is the case for domestic issues.'[148] The foreign policy élites are likely to be more concentrated in the national capital than in their domestic counterparts; this, and the smallness of their numbers, makes personal contact and informal discussion among those interested easier than in the domestic area.[149]

The non-official élites, as has been suggested, include the leading representatives of those groups concerned with the foreign policy area, both the economically interested and the more 'respectable' of the promotional groups.[150] They include also those members of the 'communications élites' who are concerned with external affairs: diplomatic and foreign correspondents from press, radio and television, recognised 'experts', and the staffs of the expanding body of non-official and semi-official research institutes and organisations in developed states.[151] The official élites include the responsible political leaders, the diplomatic services, those civil servants in other departments whose work involves them in external policy, and the senior officers of the armed forces. The political leadership forms the most crucial link between the domestic arena and the international. Its recruitment differs little, if at all, from the recruitment of domestic leaders; at the highest levels, of course, its members are responsible both for foreign and domestic policy.[152] In contrast the administrative and military élites, in most countries, are separated to a considerable degree from domestic politics. Within domestic ministries those sections concerned with international questions are commonly organised into a separate division, whose staff specialise in that division. Diplomatic services are small enough and distinctive enough to form a body with a common outlook; their pattern of recruitment and the prestige which still attaches to diplomacy make them, in many countries, an intellectual and a social élite.[153] The professional military form a coherent and disciplined group with distinctive values and attitudes, with their own conceptions of the national interest and national security. Their distinctiveness, and the complexities of their role in foreign and domestic policy, have given rise to a considerable literature on civil–military relations.[154]

The pattern of the foreign policy process differs from the pattern of politics on domestic issues in a number of ways. The executive has certain advantages which do not hold so strongly in the domestic field. The close link between the symbols of nationhood and foreign policy gives the views of the government, as representing the state, a special authority. The degree of secrecy in foreign policy, the extent of the government's superiority in its sources of information and in its control over information, is far greater than in any area of domestic politics. Consequently the executive can usually take the initiative in formulating and defining the issues as they appear in the public debate; and 'he who determines what politics is about runs the country, because the definition of the alternatives is the choice of conflicts, and the choice of conflicts allocates power'.[155]

Conversely the legislature, and unofficial organisations, suffer from a number of particular disadvantages. 'Foreign affairs is a matter for negotiation rather than legislation.'[156] It is therefore less easy for legislatures to come to grips with government proposals, or to subject them to lengthy examination and debate. While a treaty is under negotiation, ministers can turn away questions on grounds of delicacy and flexibility; when an agreement has been reached they can claim that it is too late for Parliament to amend it. The firmest hold legislatures can get on external policy is on the defence budget; though even here its examination is hampered by secrecy and by considerations of national security. Its limited access to information prevents even the most powerful legislature from taking the initiative in major issues, and forces it to rely on executive proposals.[157] Legislators' awareness of popular disinterest in foreign issues discourages them further from spending too much time on foreign affairs. For unofficial organisations, the same problem of access to information and dependence on the government as a source arises. Government awareness of the need to maintain and encourage domestic support for its policies may, indeed, on occasion reverse the process of influence, with governments encouraging and supporting the activities of groups in this field.[158] Those groups with their own sources of relevant information – business groups in the area of economic policy, church groups with their own network of international contacts, for instance – are likely to find themselves best able to influence the government.

The domestic process of foreign policy, then, constitutes a distinctive area, follows a distinctive pattern, and involves a distinctive set of actors playing distinctive roles. But it *is* a political process; and the participants in the process are drawn from a wider circle than the executive alone. Why, then, the so frequent assertion that the making of foreign policy is a matter for the executive alone? The answer must partly be, as has been suggested, the poverty of research in the foreign policy area. Partly, too, the observed advantages available to the executive in the foreign policy field encourage the assumption that its control is, for all intents and purposes, complete. Partly, it comes from the tendency to lump all foreign policy issues into a single category, and to draw one's conclusions from a study of only a section of that category.

There has been an understandable bias in the study of foreign policy towards the examination of 'great events' and major crises, to the neglect of the more regular but less crucial aspects of international relations. In a crisis, facing an urgent and fundamental decision, or under the threat of war, all the advantages are with the executive. Time is at a premium, central control most necessary; national security at stake, and national unity likely to be strongest. Non-crisis decisions are likely to follow a different pattern. 'When there is time for planning there is time for disagreement'; and disagreement 'spreads the area of involvement toward all individuals who possess or represent resources that would improve the positions of the initial combatants'.[159] National security is not at stake to the same extent in different foreign policy decisions – indeed, in some it is hardly at stake at all. The foreign policy area needs, therefore, to be further divided into a number of subsectors.

The field may broadly be divided into three levels. At the highest (the most studied level) values relevant to the whole society are at stake. National unity is therefore likely to be strongest – or, if there is disagreement, dissent is likely to be most fundamental. At this level, therefore, the executive is likely to dominate and the influence of the domestic process to be most minimal – unless public support for policy breaks down. At the middle level, of 'normal' relations and regular transactions, the values most directly at stake are those of sections of society, of interested groups. The influence of such groups, the likelihood and the potential for disagreement and manœuvring both within the executive and outside it, is therefore likely to be considerably higher. The presence of conflicting interests in many such issues will limit the influence of any one group, and create a pattern of policy-making not unlike that which holds in domestic politics. At the lowest level (of, for instance, relations with distant countries with which few domestic interests are involved) relatively few domestic values are at stake; and the process of policy-making is therefore likely to be dominated by the relevant section of the executive, or by that section in conjunction with the few domestic interests involved.[160]

At the highest level all aspects of foreign policy will be handled in a similar fashion by similar actors. Being seen to involve values relevant to the whole society, they will involve the highest political leadership and arouse interest across the whole domestic political élite. Most of the issues dealt with at this level, from the nature of the case, will be military threats to national security, or will involve a major military element; though a central economic threat to a country particularly dependent on a staple export, or a major non-military international commitment (such as a government decision to enter the E.E.C., for instance), may also be seen at this level. At the middle level, however, a considerable degree of autonomy may be discerned for particular subsectors. In many developed democratic states the external aspects of agricultural policy are dealt with by a distinctive set of actors, in comparative isolation from other areas of foreign policy.[161] Similarly, trade policy is often a semi-autonomous sector, decided between the business organisations and the trade ministry. The disarmament sector is marked by relatively clear boundaries and relative insulation from the other aspects of Soviet–American relations; and it is in the interest of both governments that this should be so.[162] At the lowest level policy may be made in almost complete isolation from other considerations, though within the overall framework of national foreign policy objectives; either because of the 'technical and bureaucratic' methods which Carl Friedrich sees as characterising this level, or because of the ability of those few interested parties to agree on policy without wider considerations being brought to bear.[163]

There is, then, a discernible domestic process in foreign policy-making, the pattern of which varies from sector to sector and level to level. In most countries it remains pre-eminently an executive process, in which non-executive elements play only a limited and subsidiary role. But the extent of executive dominance is variable; and even here, in the strongest bastion of executive control, one can discern a process of 'creeping pluralism, that is, the gradual growth of political groups especially concerned with the protection and promotion of particular interests'.[164] Even in areas where the executive retains unchallenged control of policy, domestic factors exert a clear restraint. If élite opinion and organised groups are unable to exert direct pressure on policy in the short term, if party pressure and parliamentary activity are unable to control immediate decisions, their influence in the long-term is considerable. The policy-maker is ultimately dependent on the support of his domestic political base; if that gives way, his career and his policy will collapse beneath him. In the long run, then, 'the climate in which the responsible and official officers of the Executive operate', the consensus of élite opinion, the acquiescence of the uninvolved public, the continued approval of influential interests, set recognisable limits to the policy-maker's freedom of action.[165] The cultivation of domestic support, the provision of leadership for domestic opinion, the management of domestic interests, must therefore be among the first concerns of those who are responsible for foreign policy. 'Policy faces inward as much as outward, seeking to reconcile conflicting goals, to adjust aspirations to available means, and to accommodate the different advocates of these competing goals and aspirations to one another. It is here that the essence of policy-making seems to lie, in a process that is in its deepest sense political.'[166]

5 Crossing the Boundary

Political relations between states are not exclusively intergovernmental, channelled neatly through embassies, foreign offices and ministerial contacts. The nation-state has never been as impermeable an entity, with boundaries as secure, as its apologists and theorists have argued. Interference by foreign governments in the internal affairs of other states is as old as civilisation – openly or secretly, by threat or by subsidy. Trading connections, marriage, personal acquaintance, 'the republic of letters', the fellowship of believers, have all created loyalties which crossed the boundaries of the nation-state. The modern state, with its claim to a monopoly of domestic authority and its demand for the undivided loyalty of its citizens, has never succeeded in freeing itself from the fear of external penetration or internal subversion; indeed the fear of subversion, of 'international conspiracies', masonic, Jacobin, Catholic, Jewish, Capitalist or Communist, has been a recurring factor in internal domestic politics. As we have seen, external policy has also been a perennial factor in domestic politics: the foreign expedition which makes the reputation of a politician or a general, the use of foreign policy issues for factional advantage, the problem of mobilising and maintaining domestic support for a foreign policy in the face of the burdens it imposes or the deprivations it demands.

Political interaction across the boundaries which governments attempt to maintain between states, then, is nothing new. But the range and volume of cross-national transactions in the modern international system is of an entirely different order from the relatively limited and largely inter-élite contacts of pre-modern international society. Modern mass communications have created at least the veneer of a common international culture, and provided governments with means of communicating directly with foreign populations – if necessary, through radio, without their own government's consent. Mass literacy, the cinema, radio and television, the circulation of journals and the exchange of literature, have enormously expanded popular awareness of the world beyond each nation's boundaries – of foreign governments and peoples, of foreign living standards, fashions and discontents: standards of comparison for domestic demands, or habits to be imitated within the domestic context. The advent of mass international travel, for business, study, above all for tourism, is making it increasingly difficult for governments to insulate their citizens from these foreign influences. The growth of a global economy, in which not only materials and completed manufactures but also components, capital and labour flow to and fro across state boundaries in an intricate and delicate pattern of interdependence which national governments neither control nor fully understand, has similarly blurred the distinction between the national and the international in the modern state system.

Political scientists have been slow to examine these linkages, or to absorb their significance into their organisation of political phenomena. The frameworks used to conceptualise national and international politics still largely accept the sharp boundaries between a state and its environment postulated by Plato or Hobbes, even while these boundaries become fainter and fainter. To a considerable degree we are 'the prisoners of our own concepts', reluctant to turn our attention to foreign policy and transnational phenomena because they do not fit into the traditional categories.[167] Our view may be further distorted, particularly as we apply our conceptual models to the 'non-Western' world, by our 'biased sample of political systems' and our limited model of the international system – of political systems as stable and orderly states with adequate resources for their needs, and of the international system as disorderly and unstable, both drawn from the historical experience of the European world.[168] Yet 'almost every day incidents are reported that defy the principles of sovereignty'.[169] The World Council of Churches offers support to groups working to transform the internal politics of South Africa. The European Human Rights Commission admits complaints by the Scandinavian governments against the Greek government's treatment of political prisoners, by East African Asians against the British government's denial of their entry. Belgian dockers pledge their support for British dockers against threatened diversion of trade during a strike. The Soviet premier visits Egypt to press upon its government conditions for his country's continued economic and military support – and so on. A small, but growing, number of students of domestic and international politics have therefore turned to the examination of these cross-national linkages.

Several writers have explored the social characteristics of non-governmental international contacts. Raymond Aron has described the development of 'transnational societies' in several historical international systems: a society which 'flourishes in proportion to the freedom of exchange, migration or communication, the strength of common beliefs, the number of non-national organisations, and the solemnity of collective ceremonies' allowed or encouraged by national governments.[170] Chadwick Alger has applied Almond and Coleman's model of political systems to 'the international society of individuals' constituted by those 'national officials who engage in face-to-face contact with officials of other nations and members of secretariats of international organisations' – so stressing the role of international organisations in developing the primitive institutions of this society.[171] Karl Deutsch and a number of other scholars have examined the growth of political communities above the national level, of the disappearance (as between Canada and the United States in the nineteenth century) of the expectation of possible future conflict, and of the further institutionalisation of this sense of community into successful and unsuccessful attempts at federation.[172] This in its turn has generated a considerable school of integration and interaction studies. There remain, however, a good many gaps in the application of these concepts to the activities of cross-national groups and to the nature of particular relationships.

The international corporation as a cross-national entity is now attracting considerable attention from economists and political scientists.[173] Other non-governmental organisations have as yet attracted a good deal less academic study. Churches, for instance, have a natural involvement in foreign policy, because of the global pretensions of most religions and the international links which most churches maintain; so that when Baptists are persecuted in the U.S.S.R., Catholics in Poland, or Jews in Iraq, their fellow-believers are aroused and interested. International federations of a wide range of promotional groups, concerned with aid, minority rights, the prevention of slavery or the status of women, hold consultative status with public international organisations, and co-ordinate their attempts to influence the policies of their own governments and to lobby the representatives of other states. The influence of most of these organisations may be minimal, or may be effective only on the marginal issues of international politics; but the impact of some of them, of for instance the private aid organisation on the politics of recipient states and on their own governments' attitudes to economic developments, would surely repay further study.[174]

The work of James Rosenau has provided some valuable theoretical concepts for the study of cross-national linkages, already widely influential among American and European scholars.[175] His classification of the different types of linkage processes identifies three basic types of cross-national linkages: the penetrative, the reactive and the emulative. 'A penetrative process occurs when members of one polity serve as participants in the political processes of another', whether the outside participants be an occupying army (the most extreme case), members of a foreign aid mission, representatives of an international organisation, businessmen from international companies, foreign and clandestine subversives, or members of foreign political parties or churches with domestic links.[176] The reactive process is the direct opposite to this deliberate intervention of external actors in domestic politics: the pattern of domestic responses to external actions which were not primarily intended to influence domestic politics, or which were not intended to influence domestic politics in the direction indicated by the response. A simple example of the unintended and unanticipated response would be the impact of Russian satellite development on the American educational system; of responses taking an unintended direction, hostile or nationalist reactions to a foreign aid programme. The emulative process 'is a special form of the reactive type', when the response is not only triggered off by a foreign action but takes essentially the same form as the foreign action. This is known to others as the 'demonstration' effect, a widely observed phenomenon in the modern world, in which student demonstrators or protesting farmers imitate their fellows in other countries, in which waves of hijackings, kidnappings, even self-immolation, sweep across much of the world, or in which issues such as law and order are raised in one country and rapidly taken up elsewhere.

A number of essays on particular patterns of linkage relationships suggest the possibilities for further study.[177] Two longer studies of the special case of Germany examine in some detail the patterns and structures of interaction between intra-German and international politics, emphasising the extent to which within a divided country 'the two antagonistic systems at once stand off from and penetrate each other'.[178] But in general the potential in this area, again, is much greater than the achievement so far. One hopes that more detailed case studies are projected or are under way.

The problem of sovereignty – of states' control over their national boundaries, and of their claim to supreme authority within those boundaries – recurs here. Most of those engaged in the study of linkages are agreed on the need to redefine sovereignty in relative terms. Karl Deutsch suggests that we would do better to 'describe sovereignty as an intensive type of autonomy': a relatively high ability to resist the impact of external events, and so to control the making of internal policy.[179] It follows from this that some states are more sovereign than others – that weaker states could be more accurately described, for instance, as 'pockets of semi-autonomy'. 'The smaller the human and material resources of a state the greater are the difficulties it must surmount if it is to maintain any valid political options at all and, in consequence, the smaller the state the less viable it is as a genuinely independent member of the international community.'[180] States which are deficient in internal resources, or which lack sufficient internal stability to resist external participation in their political processes, form penetrated systems.

The clearest examples of penetrated systems are to be found in the developing world.[181] But developed states, with sufficient resources to maintain their autonomy in most areas, may constitute partially penetrated systems in specific areas of weakness. This is, for instance, the position of Western European countries in defence, in which their lack of adequate resources allows the United States to play a predominant role. Deutsch points out that there is an element of voluntariness in the acceptance or rejection of external penetration. Reduction of foreign trade (or even attempts at complete autarchy), restriction of foreign travel and foreign visitors, campaigns against 'cosmopolitans' or a xenophobic atmosphere can preserve for, say, Albania or Burma more control over their internal affairs than other countries of their size.[182] But the rarity of such cases in the modern international system suggests that the advantages to be gained from accepting international links often outweigh the risks or subversion they bring with them; so that, for instance, the Communist suspicion of Western capitalists gives way little by little to the encouragement of foreign tourism in Eastern Europe and the Soviet Union, as the attraction of the foreign exchange they bring with them grows stronger.

Few of these concepts have yet entered the common discourse of political science, or been absorbed into the texts of student courses. Foreign policy indeed, in spite of the growing literature of academic study, is still something of 'a no man's land – neglected not because students of politics have thought the topic unimportant but because the divisions between the two fields have tended to foster this neglect'.[183] It is still acceptable in comparative politics to discuss and classify political systems with reference only to their internal institutions and culture, without considering the significance of their differing external situations. It is still acceptable to treat national boundaries, for purposes of political analysis, as for practical purposes crossed only by governmental decisions under governmental control; even though, in the Atlantic area particularly but also in the Communist system and in the developing world, the boundary between national and international behaviour is becoming less and less distinct. In the last few years, 'as political scientists have become increasingly concerned with the adaptation and transformation of political systems . . . there has been an increasing tendency to focus on the interaction of whole political systems with their domestic and international environments, since it is at this level that it becomes possible to explain political change'.[184] This essay has attempted to introduce and illustrate some of the academic approaches to the study of this interaction. It is to be hoped that it will encourage further study.

References

1. Thomas Hobbes, *Leviathan* (Oxford: Blackwell, 1960) chap. 18, p. 117.
2. John Locke, *The Second Treatise of Government* (Oxford: Blackwell, 1948) chap. 12, pp. 72–3.
3. U.S. Constitution, Article 2, Section 2. The American constitution limited presidential power severely even in this area, however, requiring Senatorial consent to treaty-making, and reserving to Congress the right formally to declare war and to regulate foreign commerce.
4. Translation in Appendix to Dorothy Pickles, *The Fifth French Republic*, 3rd ed. (London, 1965). It was of course part of the Gaullist view of foreign policy and of the state to give responsibility for foreign affairs to the President rather than the Prime Minister.
5. Kenneth N. Waltz, *Foreign Policy and Democratic Politics* (Boston, 1967) chap. 4, contains a critical discussion of bipartisanship in foreign policy in Britain and America.
6. Joseph Frankel, *The Making of Foreign Policy* (Oxford, 1963) pp. 20–4.
7. Wolfram F. Hanrieder, *West German Foreign Policy, 1949–1963* (Stanford, Calif., 1967) p. 7.
8. Dorothy Pickles, 'French Foreign Policy', in *The Foreign Policies of the Powers*, ed. F. S. Northedge (London, 1968) p. 187.
9. David Vital, *The Making of British Foreign Policy* (London, 1968) p. 10.
10. For a further discussion see T. B. Millar, 'On Writing about Foreign Policy', in *International Politics and Foreign Policy*, ed. James N. Rosenau, rev. ed. (New York, 1969) pp. 57–64.
11. J. P. Nettl, 'The State as a Conceptual Variable', *World Politics*, xx (1967–8) 564.
12. Arnold Wolfers, *Discord and Collaboration: Essays on International Politics* (Baltimore, 1962) chap. 1; Roy F. Jones, *Analysing Foreign Policy: An Introduction to Some Conceptual Problems* (London, 1970) chap. 6.

13. Hans J. Morgenthau, *Politics among Nations: The Struggle for Power and Peace*, 3rd ed. (New York, 1960) p. 27. For Morgenthau this is both a description of the objectives which policymakers generally follow and a recommendation of the objectives which they ought to follow.
14. F. S. Northedge, 'The Nature of Foreign Policy', in Northedge (ed.), *The Foreign Policies of the Powers*, p. 27.
15. Henry Kissinger, 'Domestic Structure and Foreign Policy', in Rosenau (ed.), *International Politics and Foreign Policy*, rev. ed., p. 261.
16. Thus Vital, in *The Making of British Foreign Policy*, includes all non-executive factors in a chapter entitled 'The Domestic Environment'. 'The making of foreign policy', he remarks, 'is the business of the Executive and for almost all practical purposes the Executive is unfettered in its exercise of this function' (p. 49).
17. Norman Kogan, *The Politics of Italian Foreign Policy* (New York, 1963) p. vii.
18. Northedge, *The Foreign Policies of the Powers*, p. 29.
19. Waltz, *Foreign Policy and Democratic Politics*, pp. 66, 67.
20. Gabriel A. Almond and James S. Coleman (eds), *The Politics of the Developing Areas* (Princeton, 1960) pp. 3–64. James N. Rosenau, in *Approaches to Comparative and International Politics*, ed. R. Barry Farrell (Evanston, Ill., 1966) pp. 58–9, provides a strong critique of 'the wide gulf that separates students of comparative and international politics' here.
21. F. H. Hinsley, 'On the Present State and the Future Development of the International System', *World Politics*, xx (1967–8) 706.
22. See, for instance, John Burton, *International Relations: A General Theory* (Cambridge, 1965) p. 245: 'The purpose of studies of International Relations is to evolve general theories which suggest policies by which peace and security may be achieved.'
23. Morgenthau, *Politics among Nations*, 3rd ed., p. 167: 'The aspiration for power on the part of several nations, each trying either to maintain or overthrow the status quo, leads *of necessity* to a configuration that is called the balance of power *and to policies that aim at preserving it*' (my italics).
24. Northedge, *The Foreign Policies of the Powers*, pp. 13, 14.
25. Vernon V. Aspaturian, 'Internal Politics and Foreign Policy

in the Soviet System', in Farrell (ed.), *Approaches to Comparative and International Politics*, p. 235.

26. Harold and Margaret Sprout, *The Ecological Perspective on Human Affairs* (Princeton, 1965) provides a review of the literature and a thorough discussion of the relationship between states and the permanent external environment.
27. Kenneth W. Thompson and Roy C. Macridis, 'The Comparative Study of Foreign Policy' in *Foreign Policy in World Politics*, ed. Roy C. Macridis, 3rd ed. (Englewood Cliffs, N. J., 1968), provide a representative list of these external factors.
28. Stanley Hoffman, 'Restraints and Choices in American Foreign Policy', in *Readings in the Making of American Foreign Policy*, ed. Andrew M. Scott and Raymond H. Dawson (New York, 1965) p. 26.
29. Morgenthau, *Politics among Nations*, 3rd ed., chaps 15–18.
30. K. J. Holsti, *International Politics: A Framework for Analysis* (Englewood Cliffs, N.J., 1967) chaps 2–3, contains a clear introduction to the concept of the international system. The analogy between the international system and anthropological studies of primitive societies is developed by Roger D. Masters in 'World Politics as a Primitive Political System', *World Politics*, XVI (1963–4) 595–619.
31. Morgenthau, *Politics among Nations*, p. 261.
32. Inis L. Claude, *The Changing United Nations* (New York, 1967) chap. 4, 'Collective Legitimization as a Political Function of the United Nations'.
33. Joseph Frankel, *International Politics: Conflict and Harmony* (London, 1969) p. 188.
34. Compare the discussions in Morgenthau, *Politics among Nations*, chap. 18, and Holsti, *International Politics*, chap. 13.
35. Karl W. Deutsch, *The Analysis of International Relations* (Englewood Cliffs, N.J., 1968) p. 162.
36. Unless, of course, it is prepared to risk or sacrifice these interests, and to ignore domestic opposition from 'interested' groups: questions which will be discussed in the two following sections. See Stanley Hoffman's discussion of the limits America's commitments and investments place on her foreign policy alternatives in Scott and Dawson, *Readings in the Making of American Foreign Policy*, pp. 28–34.
37. Geoffrey Barraclough, *An Introduction to Contemporary History* (London, 1964) traces the patterns of these developments from

the late nineteenth century to 'the "post-modern" period in which we live' (p. 15).

38. Hinsley, in *World Politics* (1967–8) p. 715.
39. Kenneth Younger, *Changing Perspectives in British Foreign Policy*, (Oxford, 1964) p. 115.
40. Burton, *International Relations*, chaps 9 and 10.
41. Alastair Buchan (ed.), *Europe's Futures, Europe's Choices* (London, 1969) p. 3. Bruce Russett, *Trends in World Politics* (New York, 1965) contains a useful introduction to the problem of politically relevant change, with some speculation as to their possible consequences for the future.
42. Deutsch, *The Analysis of International Relations*, p. 26.
43. John H. Herz, 'The Rise and Demise of the Territorial State', *World Politics*, IX (1956–7) 473–93; 'The Territorial State Revisited', in *International Politics and Foreign Policy*, ed. Rosenau, rev. ed., pp. 76–89.
44. Ernst Haas, 'International Integration: The European and The Universal Process', *International Organisation*, XV (1961) 366–92; Leon N. Lindberg, *The Political Dynamics of European Economic Integration* (Stanford, Calif., 1963).
45. Karl W. Deutsch, 'The Impact of Communications upon International Relations Theory', in *Theory of International Relations*, ed. Abdul A. Said (Englewood Cliffs, N.J., 1968).
46. For an essay on the British government's adjustment to some of these new developments, see Max Beloff, *New Dimensions in Foreign Policy: A Study in British Administrative Experience, 1947–59* (London, 1961).
47. Thompson and Macridis, in *Foreign Policy in World Politics*, ed. Macridis, pp. 17–21.
48. Max Beloff, *The Future of British Foreign Policy* (London, 1969) p. 149.
49. *Report of the Review Committee on Overseas Representation* ('The Duncan Report'), Cmnd 4107 (London, July 1969), p. 14.
50. For an informative short essay on the flow of incoming material and the process through which it is absorbed and acted upon in the U.S. Department of State, see Charlton Ogburn, Jr, 'The Flow of Policy Making in the Department of State', reprinted in Scott and Dawson, *Readings in the Making of American Foreign Policy*, and in Burton M. Sapin, *The Making of United States Foreign Policy* (Washington and New York, 1966).

51. Lord Strang (and others), *The Foreign Office* (London, 1955) p. 116.
52. For a major power with global interests this organisational system has very considerable dimensions. Karl Deutsch estimates (in *Analysis of International Relations*, p. 95) that the U.S. State Department and its associated agencies (concerned with aid, information and disarmament) employ some 10,000 people in Washington and a further 40,000 abroad. To these must be added the independent intelligence agencies, the policy divisions of the Department of Defense, the international divisions of the Department of Commerce and the U.S. Treasury, and the co-ordinating machinery of the National Security Council and the White House staff.
53. Sapin, *The Making of United States Foreign Policy*, p. 31.
54. This is the theme of Sapin's study, though he doubts (p. 11) whether there is any 'set of organisational arrangements and relationships ideally suited to meet the needs of the foreign policy organisation'. Beloff in *The Future of British Foreign Policy* (p. 144) similarly asserts that: 'The organisation of the British government for the purpose of foreign affairs is . . . a subject of direct consequence for policy.'
55. Vital, *The Making of British Foreign Policy*, p. 96.
56. Deutsch, *Analysis of International Relations*, p. 124.
57. Richard C. Snyder, H. W. Bruck and Burton Sapin, *Foreign Policy Decision-Making* (Glencoe, Ill., 1962) p. 59.
58. The importance of the flow of communication, of the ability of policy-making structures to process the fluctuating flow of incoming messages, and of the problem of 'overload' under crisis conditions, is developed in Karl W. Deutsch, *The Nerves of Government* (Glencoe, Ill., 1963) pt iii.
59. Charles E. Lindblom, *The Policy-Making Process* (Englewood Cliffs, N.J., 1968) pp. 23–4.
60. Wolfers, *Discord and Collaboration*, p. 39, notes the degree to which belief in the importance of economic factors has guided Soviet foreign policy, while Franklin Roosevelt was guided by his belief in the importance of personal relationships in dealing with Stalin, and Hitler by his belief in the significance of geography in his expansionist calculations towards the East.
61. Perhaps the most classic public exposition of such a view was 'The Sources of Soviet Conduct' by George Kennan, originally published in *Foreign Affairs*, xxv (1947) 556–82, providing an

interpretation of the motives and pressures behind Soviet foreign policy and a set of recommendations for the American response.

62. President de Gaulle, for instance, was not only clear but publicly explicit about his understanding of the 'realities' of the international system, of the nature of French interests, and of her proper role in the world.
63. There is a considerable literature on capabilities and resources. For a simple introduction see Deutsch, *Analysis of International Relations*, chap. 3.
64. The essay is reprinted in full in Snyder, Bruck and Sapin, *Foreign Policy Decision-Making*, pp. 14–185.
65. Ibid., p. 67.
66. The most thoroughgoing application of the decision-making scheme so far is to be found in Glenn D. Paige, *The Korean Decision* (New York, 1968).
67. Op. cit., p. 9.
68. George Modelski, *A Theory of Foreign Policy* (Princeton, 1962) pp. 13, 14.
69. Jones, *Analysing Foreign Policy*, p. 40. The case-study literature in the foreign policy field reflects the attraction of major crises, or of decisions which can be described (at least in hindsight) as 'historic', for the student; so focusing on the outbreak of the Korean War or of the First World War, the American decision to aid Greece and Turkey, the Cuban crisis, or the British decision to apply to the E.E.C.
70. Vital, *The Making of British Foreign Policy*, pp. 104–9.
71. Deutsch, *Analysis of International Relations*, chap. 8; more fully set out in *The Nerves of Government*.
72. Charles E. Lindblom, *The Intelligence of Democracy: Decision-Making by Mutual Adjustment* (New York, 1970); J. G. March and Herbert A. Simon, *Organisations* (New York, 1958).
73. Rosenau in Farrell (ed.), *Approaches to Comparative and International Politics*, p. 32.
74. Walter Lippmann, *The Public Philosophy* (New York, 1955) p. 13.
75. The concept is briefly and clearly examined by James Rosenau in the *International Encyclopedia of Social Sciences* (New York, 1968), under the heading 'National Interest'; and more extensively explored by Joseph Frankel in *National Interest* (London, 1970).
76. Morgenthau, *Politics among Nations*, p. 7.

77. Burton, *International Relations*, p. 54. Charles A. McClelland, *Theory and the International System* (New York, 1966) chap. 3, gives a concise and thorough critique of the realists' concept of power.
78. Though Sapin in *The Making of United States Foreign Policy*, p. 2, defines foreign policy, with defence policy, as 'subcategories of national security policy'.
79. Macridis, 'French Foreign Policy', in Macridis (ed.), *Foreign Policy in World Politics*, p. 73; Kogan, *The Politics of Italian Foreign Policy*, p. 36.
80. Adam B. Ulam, *Expansion and Coexistence: The History of Soviet Foreign Policy, 1917–1967* (London, 1968) p. 347; Kogan, *The Politics of Italian Foreign Policy*, p. 143.
81. Though Thompson and Macridis in the introduction to *Foreign Policy in World Politics*, p. 2, assume them to be so: 'Not only are the interests of a nation permanent in character, but they range themselves in a hierarchy of greater and lesser interests.' If only it were so simple!
82. The difficult question of motivation and values is discussed in Snyder, Bruck and Sapin, *Foreign Policy Decision-Making*, pp. 137–60, and in Frankel, *The Making of Foreign Policy*, chaps. 8–10.
83. Adda B. Bozeman, *Politics and Culture in International History* (Princeton, N.J., 1960), and a number of essays in Joel Larus (ed.), *Comparative World Politics: Readings in Western and Premodern Non-Western International Relations* (Belmont, Calif., 1964), explore this cultural dimension.
84. Frankel, *The Making of Foreign Policy*, p. 168.
85. The problem of rationality and perception is explored further in two articles reprinted in Rosenau (ed.), *International Politics and Foreign Policy*: 'Assumptions of Rationality and Non-Rationality in Models of the International System' by Sidney Verba (also in *The International System*, ed. Klaus Knorr and Sidney Verba (Princeton, 1961)), and 'Hypotheses on Misperception' by Robert Jervis (also in *World Politics*, xx (1968)).
86. Frankel, *The Making of Foreign Policy*, p. 55, distinguishes between the decision-maker's subjective 'psychological environment' and the 'operational' environment as perceived by 'the omniscient observer'. But few academics, one hopes, would claim omniscience.
87. Stanley Hoffman, 'International Relations: The Long Road to Theory', *World Politics*, XI (1959) 366. Compare with Sir William Hayter's comment in *Russia and the World: A Study*

of Soviet Foreign Policy (London, 1970) p. 23, that 'some of the disadvantages from which the Soviet diplomat suffers' stem from his ideological inability to 'look objectively at the country on which he is reporting or the people with whom he is negotiating'.

88. Wolfers, *Discord and Collaboration*, p. 71.
89. Holsti in *International Politics*, pp. 131–46, provides an alternative classification, into 'core' interests and values, middle-range goals and long-term objectives: self-preservation and survival, economic, territorial and prestige goals, and ideas about the organisation of the international system and a country's role in that system.
90. Wolfers, *Discord and Collaboration*, pp. 73–80.
91. Note that it is not only these private, indirect goals which conflict with each other. Vital in *The Making of British Foreign Policy*, p. 31, argues that 'the really crucial policy dilemmas for contemporary Britain arise out of the degree to which the pursuit of national security (conceived in politico-military terms) and the pursuit of national welfare (conceived in socio-economic terms) have turned out to be significantly – though perhaps not wholly – incompatible with each other'.
92. Senator James Fulbright, *Old Myths and New Realities* (New York, 1965).
93. Macridis in *Foreign Policy in World Politics*, p. 66; Beloff in *The Future of British Foreign Policy*, p. 4.
94. The reader will recognise that this distinction between myth and reality bears a certain similarity to the distinction the realist school makes between national interest and 'ideology'. An interesting discussion, in African terms, of the difficulty of distinguishing between these is to be found in William Zartmann, 'National Interest and Ideology', in *African Diplomacy*, ed. Vernon McKay (New York, 1966).
95. Vital, *The Making of British Foreign Policy*, pp. 98–9; Waltz, *Foreign Policy and Democratic Politics*, chap. 1.
96. Macridis in *Foreign Policy in World Politics*, p. 62.
97. The constant concern of critics with the need for 'planning' in foreign policy reflects, in part, their recognition of the tendency for policy-makers to follow implicit (and often outdated) assumptions rather than to formulate explicit objectives. See, for instance, the contributions of W. W. Rostow, Dean Rusk and Henry A. Kissinger in Scott and Dawson, *Readings in the Making of American Foreign Policy*.

98. McClelland, *Theory and the International System*, chap. 5, provides a simple introduction to the concepts involved; the fullest development of the approach is Karl Deutsch's *The Nerves of Government*.

99. Karl Deutsch, 'Toward an Inventory of Basic Trends and Patterns in Comparative and International Politics', in *International Politics and Foreign Policy*, pp. 498–512 (originally published in *American Political Science Review*, LIV (1960)); Bruce Russett *et al.*, *World Handbook of Political and Social Indicators* (New Haven, 1964).

100. Thomas Schelling, 'Experimental Games and Bargaining Theory', in *The International System*, ed. Knorr and Verba.

101. William D. Coplin, 'The Impact of Simulation on Theory of International Relations', in *Theory of International Relations*, ed. Abdul A. Said (Englewood Cliffs, N.J., 1968) provides a useful short introduction for the layman.

102. John C. Harsany, 'Game Theory and the Analysis of International Conflict' in *International Politics and Foreign Policy*, p. 379.

103. Urs Schwartz, in *American Strategy: A New Perspective* (London, 1965) chap. 7, gives an approving survey of the U.S. Government's application of 'advanced thought' to its defence and foreign policies, citing their handling of the Cuban crisis and the Gulf of Tonkin as successful examples. David W. Tarr, in *American Strategy in the Nuclear Age* (New York, 1966) pp. 125–34, is less confident of the appropriateness of their application in the Vietnam conflict.

104. Michael H. Banks *et al.*, 'Gaming and Simulation in International Relations', *Political Studies*, XVI (1968) 15.

105. Nigel Forward, *The Field of Nations: An Account of Some New Approaches to International Relations* (London, 1971), contains a comprehensive, if at times rather mathematical, survey of these techniques, a full bibliography, and a light-hearted portrayal of their future use by a British government.

106. A. J. P. Taylor, *English History 1914–1945* (Oxford, 1965) p. 3.

107. H. J. Hanham (ed.), *The Nineteenth Century Constitution 1815–1914* (Cambridge, 1969) p. 56.

108. Deutsch, *Analysis of International Relations*, chap. 3.

109. Ibid., p. 38.

110. Roy C. Macridis, *Modern European Governments: Cases in Comparative Policy-Making* (Englewood Cliffs, N.J., 1968) p. 9.

111. McGeorge Bundy, quoted in *Domestic Sources of Foreign Policy*, ed. James N. Rosenau (New York, 1967) p. 4.
112. Rosenau in Farrell (ed.), *Approaches to Comparative and International Politics*, p. 39.
113. James N. Rosenau, 'Foreign Policy as an Issue Area', *Domestic Sources of Foreign Policy*, pp. 11–50. Rosenau takes the concept of 'issue area' from Robert Dahl, *Who Governs?* (New Haven, 1961).
114. The relationship between these issues is much clearer in the Soviet Union than in the United States, because of the less developed structure of the Soviet political process. See Carl Linden, *Kruschev and the Soviet Leadership* (Baltimore, Md., 1966) esp. chap. 9.
115. Here, of course, the United States is the best documented. Douglass Cater, *Power in Washington* (New York, 1964) chap. 2.
116. Vernon V. Aspaturian, 'Internal Politics and Foreign Policy in the Soviet System', *Approaches to Comparative and International Politics*, ed. Farrell, pp. 269–80.
117. Oliver Benson, 'Challenges for Research in International Relations and Comparative Politics', ibid., p. 345.
118. Kogan, *Politics of Italian Foreign Policy*, p. 50. Much the same might be said of South African foreign policy.
119. Ulam, *Expansion and Coexistence*, pp. 347, 606.
120. Ibid., p. 403.
121. Karl Kaiser, *German Foreign Policy in Transition* (Oxford, 1968) p. 35.
122. For instance, 'one may speculate that if there had been no massive threat to Israel's existence, the several social conflicts which have thus far been contained might well have proved uncontainable'. Leonard J. Fein, *Politics in Israel* (Boston, 1967) p. 209.
123. This was clearly a factor in Stalin's evocation of external enemies, as in the Communist Chinese evocation of American imperialism; and also in Sukarno's use of 'confrontation' in Indonesia.
124. 'Since 1950, foreign policy has become a vital part of the political battlefield in Japan, probably the most vital part'. Robert A. Scalapino, 'The Foreign Policy of Modern Japan', *Foreign Policy in World Politics*, ed. Macridis, p. 299.
125. Peter G. Richards, *Parliament and Foreign Affairs* (London, 1967) chap. 2, briefly surveys the movement for popular control of foreign policy in Britain.

126. Geoffrey Goodwin, *Britain and the United Nations* (Oxford, 1957) p. 422.
127. 'Never was there a clearer case of a war brought about by public opinion.' Dexter Perkins, *The Evolution of American Foreign Policy* (Oxford, 1948; 2nd ed., 1966) p. 41.
128. A. J. P. Taylor, *English History 1914–1945*, p. 386, cites both Baldwin and Dalton, for example, as excusing British acquiescence in the German reoccupation of the Rhineland on the grounds that 'public opinion would not allow it'.
129. See, for instance, R. B. McCallum, *Public Opinion and the Last Peace* (Oxford, 1944), or George Kennan, *American Diplomacy 1900–1950* (Chicago, 1951); Gabriel Almond, *The American People and Foreign Policy* (New York, 1950).
130. See, for instance, Karl W. Deutsch and Lewis J. Edinger, *Germany Rejoins the Powers: Mass Opinion, Interest Groups and Elites in Contemporary German Foreign Policy* (Stanford, Calif., 1959). James N. Rosenau's *Public Opinion and Foreign Policy* (New York, 1961), which grew out of a White House conference on public support for foreign aid, contains a useful bibliography on academic studies in the 1950s.
131. Bernard C. Cohen, 'Foreign Policy', in *International Encyclopaedia of Social Science* (New York, 1968).
132. Rosenau, 'Foreign Policy as an Issue Area', in *Domestic Sources of Foreign Policy*, pp. 28–9.
133. Ibid., pp. 36–42; Rosenau, *Public Opinion and Foreign Policy*, chap. 4.
134. Roger Hilsman, *To Move a Nation: The Politics of Foreign Policy in the Administration of John F. Kennedy* (New York, 1967) p. 542.
135. Rosenau, *Public Opinion and Foreign Policy*, p. 41.
136. Macridis in *Foreign Policy in World Politics*, pp. 75–6. Jean Blondel and E. D. Godfrey in *The Government of France* (London, 1968) p. 179, note the extent to which de Gaulle's policies on Europe were limited by French public support for the European idea and the E.E.C.
137. Scalapino, 'The Foreign Policy of Modern Japan', in *Foreign Policy in World Politics*, pp. 299–300.
138. Kenneth Younger, 'Public Opinion and British Foreign Policy', *International Affairs*, XL (1964) 24.
139. Deutsch, *Analysis of International Relations*, pp. 148–9.
140. Thompson and Macridis in *Foreign Policy in World Politics*, p. 22.

141. Macridis, *Modern European Governments*, p. 9.

142. Allen Potter, *Organised Groups in British National Politics* (London, 1961) p. 39. The Anti-Corn Law League was not, of course, a purely promotional group; there were also industrial interests at stake.

143. Bernard C. Cohen, 'The Influence of Non-Governmental Groups on Foreign Policy-Making', in *Readings in the Making of American Foreign Policy*, ed. Scott and Dawson, p. 101.

144. Lester W. Milbrath, 'Interest Groups and Foreign Policy', in *Domestic Sources of Foreign Policy*, p. 251.

145. Kogan, *Politics of Italian Foreign Policy*, chaps. 7 and 8, is, however, illuminating on the influence of the Church and of business on Italian foreign policy.

146. Potter, *Organised Groups in British National Politics*, p. 154: 'The British Government also contributes to "anglophile societies" abroad.'

147. Milbrath in *Domestic Sources of Foreign Policy*, p. 245.

148. Rosenau, ibid., p. 41.

149. 'The debate which precedes or accompanies the formulation of any move in British foreign policy', for instance, 'takes place as much in private as in public.' D. C. Watt, *Personalities and Policies: Studies in the Formulation of British Foreign Policy in the Twentieth Century* (London, 1965) p. 12.

150. Potter, *Organised Groups in British National Politics*, pp. 224–5, notes a number of promotional groups 'whose competence is recognised by the Government' to whom access to the Foreign Office is regularly granted. Some foreign policy promotional groups are in effect élite organisations, set up to 'influence the influential', with Government approval and support. Lord Windlesham, *Communication and Political Power* (London, 1966) p. 166 (in an excellent chapter on the Common Market 'campaigns' in Britain, 1961–3).

151. I am following Gabriel Almond's classification in this paragraph in *The American People and Foreign Policy*, chap. 7. An alternative classification, of the British foreign policy élite, is given in Watt, *Personalities and Policies*, chap. 1; curiously, it does not include the economically interested in the non-official élite.

152. Kissinger, in *International Politics and Foreign Policy*, pp. 267–73, draws some interesting conclusions on the relationship between the style of states' foreign policies and their patterns of leadership recruitment.

153. The Japanese Foreign Office has 'less than 2000 men of civil service rank'. Scalapino in *Foreign Policy in World Politics*, p. 297. The French foreign service has 'a hard core of some 4000 foreign service officers'; less than 5 per cent of the applicants pass the entrance examination (ibid., p. 77). The British Diplomatic Service has 1100 Administrative Class, and 1600 Executive Class, members in London and abroad (Cmnd 4107, 1969, p. 56). Over a third of the senior personnel of the Italian diplomatic service in 1957 held titles of nobility (Kogan, *Politics of Italian Foreign Policy*, p. 111). The American and the Russian foreign services, however, lack the social status and the intellectual standing which so many of their counterparts enjoy.
154. For an introduction to this extensive field, see Jacques Van Doorn (ed.) *Armed Forces and Society* (The Hague, 1968).
155. E. E. Schattschneider, 'Intensity, Visibility, Direction and Scope', *American Political Science Review*, LI (1957) 937; quoted in James A. Robinson, *Congress and Foreign Policy-Making*, rev. ed. (Homewood, Ill., 1967) p. 69.
156. Richards, *Parliament and Foreign Affairs*, p. 78.
157. The 'major themes' of Robinson's study of the U.S. Congress are its reliance on presidential initiatives and 'the changing character of information and intelligence in modern policy-making'. *Congress and Foreign Policy Making*, p. vii.
158. William Wallace, 'The Role of Interest Groups', in *The Management of Britain's External Relations*, ed. Robert Boardman and A. J. R. Groom (London, forthcoming).
159. Theodore J. Lowi, 'Making Democracy Safe for the World', in *Domestic Sources of Foreign Policy*, p. 302. It may be remarked that this is likely to hold true as much in non-democratic states as in democratic.
160. In this paragraph I am following Lowi's framework, in *Domestic Sources of Foreign Policy*, pp. 295–331. A not dissimilar framework is suggested by C. J. Friedrich, 'International Politics and Foreign Policy in Developed (Western) Systems', in *Approaches to Comparative and International Politics*, ed. Farrell, pp. 108–9. Lowi develops his framework more fully in 'American Business, Public Policy, Case Studies, and Political Theory', *World Politics*, XVI (1963–4) 677–715, and argues for its applicability to other areas of the political process as well.
161. In Italy the farm organisations exercise 'a very strong influence

over the nomination of the minister, and watchfulness to ensure that the Ministry of Agriculture rather than the Foreign Office dominates foreign agricultural policy'; while the head of the main farm organisation 'cares nothing about other areas of foreign policy'. Kogan, *Politics of Italian Foreign Policy*, p. 104.

162. Rosenau in *Approaches to Comparative and International Politics*, pp. 79–80.
163. Friedrich, ibid., p. 109. Douglass Cater's description of 'the subgovernment of sugar' in *Power in Washington*, pp. 17–20, is an interesting example of an issue (the U.S. sugar quota) which had successfully been isolated at this level until invaded by wider considerations of U.S. policy towards Latin America.
164. J. L. Freeman, *The Political Process*, rev. ed. (New York, 1965) p.5.
165. Vital, *The Making of British Foreign Policy*, p. 50.
166. Hilsman, *To Move a Nation*, p. 13.
167. Roland Young, 'Political and Legal Systems of Order', in Farrell (ed.), *Approaches to Comparative and International Politics*, p. 293.
168. Chadwick Alger, 'Comparison of Intranational and International Politics', ibid., p. 304.
169. James N. Rosenau, 'Political Science in a Shrinking World', in James N. Rosenau (ed.), *Linkage Politics* (New York, 1969) p. 2.
170. Raymond Aron, *Peace and War: A Theory of International Relations* (New York, 1966) p. 105. The concept is developed further by Karl Kaiser in 'The Interaction of Regional Subsystems', *World Politics*, XXI (1968–9) 84–107.
171. Chadwick Alger in Farrell (ed.), *Approaches to Comparative and International Politics*, p. 307 and *passim*.
172. Deutsch's framework is most clearly set out in *Political Community and the North Atlantic Area* (Princeton, 1957). The by now considerable literature on the European Communities as a potentially far-reaching example of transnational integration so far contains little on the links between the developing supranational community and the domestic politics of the member states. See, however, Helen Wallace, 'The Impact of the European Communities on National Policy-Making', *Government and Opposition* (autumn 1971).
173. See, for instance, J. N. Behrman, *National Interests and the Multi-National Enterprise* (Englewood Cliffs, N.J., 1970), or C. P. Kindleberger, *American Business Abroad* (New Haven, Conn., 1969).

174. Jeffrey Harrod, 'Non-Governmental Organisations and the Third World', *Year Book of World Affairs*, xxiv (London, 1970), provides a short and critical survey of some of the field.
175. See particularly his essay in Farrell (ed.), *Approaches to Comparative and International Politics*, his second essay in *Linkage Politics*, 'Toward the Study of National-International Linkages', and his 'Intervention as a Scientific Concept', *Journal of Conflict Resolution*, xiii (1969) 149–71.
176. *Linkage Politics*, p. 46. Max Beloff in 'Reflections on Intervention', in *The Intellectual in Politics* (London, 1970) pp. 225–234, emphasises that this form of linkage is not peculiar to modern international politics: that 'intervention is one of the instruments employed in *any* competitive international system', from the ancient world to the present.
177. See, for instance, R. V. Burks, 'The Communist Polities of Eastern Europe', and Douglas A. Chalmers, 'Developing on the Periphery: External Factors in Latin American Politics', in *Linkage Politics*; or Fred W. Riggs's earlier essay, 'The Theory of Developing Politics', *World Politics*, xvi (1963–4) 146–71.
178. Karl Kaiser, *German Foreign Policy in Transition* (Oxford, 1968) p. 130; Hanrieder, *West German Foreign Policy 1949–1963*, particularly the concluding chapter.
179. 'External Influences on the Internal Behaviour of States,' in Farrell (ed.), *Approaches to Comparative and International Politics*, p. 7.
180. David Vital, *The Inequality of States* (Oxford, 1967) p. 3. Vital points out, however, that the relationship between available resources and autonomy is not one-to-one: the internal stability of the state, and above all the presence, absence or strength of external threats, also affect the degree of viability and autonomy.
181. Edward L. Morse, 'The Transformation of Foreign Policies: Modernisation, Interdependence, and Externalisation', *World Politics*, xxii (1969–70) 371–92.
182. Deutsch in Farrell (ed.), *Approaches to Comparative and International Politics*, p. 10. South Africa's reluctance to allow the establishment of television within her frontiers, and her strict film censorship, provide a milder form of the same resistance to the penetration of external influences.
183. Farrell, *Approaches to Comparative and Internal Politics*, p. vi.
184. Gabriel A. Almond, 'Politics, Comparative', in *International Encyclopaedia of the Social Sciences*, speculating on 'the future of the comparative politics movement'.

Bibliography

The reader should find sufficient references to pursue his interests further in the endnotes to the relevant section of the text. This short bibliography is intended as a checklist for easy reference. It does not include all those works noted earlier. The intention here is to list some of the most central, and to note a few additional studies which have not found a place in the text.

1. *General Approaches*

George Modelski, *A Theory of Foreign Policy* (Princeton, 1962).

Richard C. Snyder, H. W. Bruck and Burton Sapin, *Foreign Policy Decision-Making* (Glencoe, Ill., 1962).

These two 'classical' frameworks for the study of foreign policy were written in the mid-fifties. Modelski's essay is a useful point of reference, but does not provide a very firm guide. Snyder, Bruck and Sapin's essay is ambitious and complex, aiming to include all relevant factors in its scheme. Printed with it in this volume are a number of essays criticising or expanding on the scheme.

Joseph Frankel, *The Making of Foreign Policy* (Oxford, 1963), is less ambitious than Snyder, Bruck and Sapin in model-building. It, too, discusses the whole range of relevant factors (in language which European students will find easier to grasp, and with rather more concrete examples to substantiate the points made), giving particular attention to the problems of objectives, values and rationality.

R. B. Farrell (ed.), *Approaches to Comparative and International Politics* (Evanston, Ill., 1966).

James N. Rosenau (ed.), *Domestic Sources of Foreign Policy* (New York, 1967).

James N. Rosenau (ed.), *Linkage Politics: Essays on the Convergence of National and International Systems* (New York, 1969).

These three collections of essays stem from a series of conferences of American academics. Within their different foci they represent some of the most useful and stimulating studies at present available in this area. *Domestic Sources* limits its attention to the United States (with the exception of an essay on Norwegian attitudes to foreign policy); the other two books are comparative.

2. *The International Context*

K. J. Holsti, *International Politics: A Framework for Analysis*, (Englewood Cliffs, N.J., 1967).

Karl W. Deutsch, *The Analysis of International Relations* (Englewood Cliffs, N.J., 1968).

Hans J. Morgenthau, *Politics among Nations: The Struggle for Power and Peace*, 3rd ed. (New York, 1960); 4th ed. (New York, 1967).

The student of comparative politics looking for an introduction to international politics is faced with a wide choice of texts. I would recommend Holsti as a first guide, providing a clear introduction to the concept of the international system in its first three chapters, and paying particular attention to foreign policy objectives and instruments in succeeding chapters. Deutsch's book is shorter (and cheaper) and devotes rather more attention than Holsti to domestic factors in foreign policy. Morgenthau's classic study was originally written in 1948, though extensively revised since; the reader will find this a much more 'traditional' approach.

James N. Rosenau (ed.), *International Politics and Foreign Policy: A Reader in Research and Theory*, rev. ed. (New York, 1969).

Charles A. McClelland, *Theory and the International System* (New York, 1966).

The fifty-seven articles in the Rosenau reader cover almost all the main current approaches to International Politics, though it is rather thin on the area of foreign policy-making.

McClelland's short essay is, in my view, the best available introduction to theories of international politics.

Arnold Wolfers, *Discord and Collaboration: Essays on International Politics* (Baltimore, 1962).

Charles Burton Marshall, *The Exercise of Sovereignty: Papers on Foreign Policy* (Baltimore, 1965).

Roger Hilsman and Robert C. Good (eds), *Foreign Policy in the Sixties: The Issues and the Instruments* (Baltimore, 1965).

These three collections of essays, though centred primarily on the American situation and experience, contain some stimulating insights into a number of aspects of foreign policy and international politics which are of much wider relevance. They share an approach which combines practical concern with an interest in theoretical implications.

3. *Country Studies*

The material available in English, as has already been noted, is far more plentiful on the United States than on any other country; indeed, for some important countries there is almost nothing available on the making of foreign policy itself. What is offered here is an introductory list, books covering several countries first, then those on the United States, then Britain, then other countries.

F. S. Northedge (ed.), *The Foreign Policies of the Powers* (London, 1968). Essays on the United States, Britain, France, Germany, the Soviet Union, China and India.

Roy C. Macridis (ed.), *Foreign Policy in World Politics*, 3rd ed. (Englewood Cliffs, N.J., 1968). Essays on the United States, Britain, France, Germany, the Soviet Union, 'The Soviet Union and International Communism', China, India, Japan and 'Foreign Policies in Latin America'.

Roy C. Macridis (ed.), *Modern European Governments: Cases in Comparative Policy-Making* (Englewood Cliffs, N.J., 1968). Two essays each on cases in foreign policy-making in Britain, France, Germany, and the Soviet Union.

Kenneth N. Waltz, *Foreign Policy and Democratic Politics* (Boston, 1967). A comparative study of the 'foreign policy capabilities' of Britain and the United States, which covers the impact of their differing institutions and political styles on policy-making, and includes chapters on particular areas of policy.

Richard E. Neustadt, *Alliance Politics* (New York, 1970). A short and provocative study of Anglo-American relations, focusing on the Suez crisis and the Skybolt 'affair', its theme the difficulties caused between allies by differing domestic constraints on foreign policy behaviour.

Karl Kaiser and Roger Morgan (eds), *Britain and West Germany: Changing Societies and the Future of Foreign Policy* (Oxford, 1971). This includes a full bibliography for further reading on British and German foreign policy.

Burton M. Sapin, *The Making of United States Foreign Policy* (Washington and New York, 1966).

Andrew M. Scott and Raymond H. Dawson, *Readings in the Making of American Foreign Policy* (New York, 1965).

Robert A. Dahl, *Congress and Foreign Policy* (New York, 1950).

James A. Robinson, *Congress and Foreign Policy-Making* (Homewood, Ill., 1962, 1967).

Holbert N. Carroll, 'The Congress and National Security Policy', in *The Congress and America's Future*, ed. David B. Truman (Englewood Cliffs, N.J., 1965).

Gabriel A. Almond, *The American People and Foreign Policy* (New York, 1950).

James N. Rosenau, *Public Opinion and Foreign Policy* (New York, 1961).

Eugene B. Skolnikoff, *Science, Technology and American Foreign Policy* (Cambridge, Mass., 1967). An interesting study of a number of the newer areas of concern to foreign policy-makers.

David Vital, *The Making of British Foreign Policy* (London, 1968).

Lord Strang (and others), *The Foreign Office* (London, 1955).

Robert Boardman and A. J. R. Groom (eds), *The Management of Britain's External Relations* (London, forthcoming).

Peter G. Richards, *Parliament and Foreign Affairs* (London, 1967).

Adam B. Ulam, *Expansion and Coexistence: The History of Soviet Foreign Policy (1917–1967)* (London, 1968). As its name implies, a basically historical study, and a very lengthy book, which contains, however, a good deal of useful material on policy-making.

Wolfram F. Hanrieder, *West German Foreign Policy 1949–1963* (Stanford, Calif., 1967). As much historical as analytical, but containing some very useful chapters on 'the domestic political struggle over the content and direction of West German foreign policy'.

Karl Kaiser, *German Foreign Policy in Transition: Bonn between East and West* (Oxford, 1968).

Norman Kogan, *The Politics of Italian Foreign Policy* (New York, 1963).

R. Barry Farrell, *The Making of Canadian Foreign Policy* (Englewood Cliffs, N.J., 1969).

I. William Zartmann, *International Relations in the New Africa* (Englewood Cliffs, N.J., 1966). A useful introduction to foreign policy attitudes and policy-making in the new states of Africa.

Vernon McKay (ed.), *African Diplomacy: Studies in the Determinants of Foreign Policy* (New York, 1966).

DATE DUE

FEB 5 1980		FEB 28 1980	
NOV 12 1981			
DEC 4 1981			
FEB 3 1986		FEB 1? 1986	
OCT 7 1986		MAR 31 1987	

261-2500

Printed in USA